Pure Poett

PURE POETT

The memoirs of
GENERAL SIR NIGEL POETT
KCB, DSO and bar

LEO COOPER
LONDON

First published in Great Britain in 1991 by
LEO COOPER
190 Shaftesbury Avenue, London WC2H 8JL
an imprint of Pen & Sword Books Ltd.,
47 Church Street, Barnsley, S. Yorks S70 2AS

A CIP catalogue record for this book is available
from the British Library

ISBN: 0 08052 339 7

Printed in Great Britain by Redwood Press, Melksham

*To
My Wife
who made my
Army Life
such
a Happy One*

Contents

INTRODUCTION

I have been bullied by my children and others into passing on a few of the experiences of my life. My family know how much I have enjoyed myself. I hope that this account will show some of the reasons.

My grandfather was a consultant physician. After his first wife died, he retired and travelled. He went first to Chile where he married again. His second wife was Mary McMichael who became my grandmother. After a few years in Chile, he went on to California and arrived there in 1849. In California, his ship was delayed because of the Gold Rush and the crew deserted.

My grandfather then bought some land at San Mateo, near San Francisco and lived there for a number of years. He had with him the children of his first marriage. By now they were grown up. They all married in California and settled there. As a result I have many American relations in that State.

In about 1856 my grandfather returned to England and lived at Richmond, near London. My father was born there in 1858. He was educated at Beaumont College, Windsor, and then went to the Royal Military College at Sandhurst. He was commissioned in 1876 into the 39th Regiment of Foot, The Dorsetshire Regiment.

In 1880 he saw service in the Afghan War of 1876 and then in the Bechuanaland Expedition of 1884. Later that year he was with Methuen's Horse in South Africa.

In 1890 he qualified at the Staff College at Camberley and then, in 1892, went on to become an Instructor at the R.M.C. Sandhurst. While on holiday in Dresden he met my mother, Julia Caswell, an American from Providence, Rhode Island. They were married in 1889. My eldest sister Phyllis was born in 1890 when the family was at Sandhurst, my sister Elizabeth followed in 1892 and then Evelyn in 1895.

Other Staff appointments followed Sandhurst, then a spell of Regimental Duty. In 1899 the Boer War broke out and my father was posted to Lord Roberts' staff. He continued on the GHQ staff when Lord Kitchener took over command. By the end of the war, he had become Assistant Adjutant General, gained three Mentions in Despatches and was made a Companion of the Bath. He had been awarded the Queen's South Africa Medal with four clasps and the King's South Africa Medal with two clasps. He had also been appointed a Brevet Lieutenant-Colonel.

My father now found himself appointed to the same staff post under Lord Kitchener's successor. This was not at all what he wanted. Command of the 1st Battalion of the Dorsetshire Regiment was about to come up and that was what he hoped for. The C-in-C supported him and, in due course, he was selected to command the Battalion which was then in India. My father much enjoyed his period in command and has written in detail about it. His memoirs have been serialized in the magazine, *The Great War*, 1989 and 1990 editions. His family had accompanied him to India and much enjoyed it there. In 1907 he was promoted Brigadier-General and served first as Deputy Adjutant General and then Chief of Staff, Eastern Command, India. 1907 was also the year in which my twin sister Angela and I were born.

When my mother realized that she was going to have another baby she left for England. My father remained in India and the family rented Rew House, at Winterborne St Martin close to Dorchester.

On 20 August, 1907, we twins appeared. Angela was slightly ahead of me. There was great jubilation in the family to have a boy at last. Angela was a sturdy baby from the outset but I was a weakly one. However, all possible care was lavished on me and I soon became a healthy child.

CHAPTER I

Growing Up

The family returned to India shortly after the birth of the twins. I have no recollection of this period of my life, but in my father's memoirs he has left a detailed and interesting account. By 1910 he had spent a great many years abroad, particularly in India. He now had an urge to start a new life and fancied farming in British Columbia.

The Canadian Pacific Railway at that time was offering attractive terms for the purchase of land. Like many soldiers my father had a longing for a property of his own. His family also welcomed the idea of settling down. Accordingly when his staff appointment, which had already been extended for a year, was completed, he sent in his papers and left for home with his family.

In due course the purchase of a suitable property was negotiated and we moved to Canada. At that time my twin and I were four years old. The property was near Lake Windermere in a very beautiful district of the Rockies. The CPR had indicated their intention of building a railway close to the property which would increase its value.

The family settled down well with pleasant neighbours and lots to do. We children enjoyed the winter season with its tobogganing, skating and so on. In the summer, there were picnics and bathing.

When my father went to Canada he was 54 years old and he found the manual work hard. Sufficient help was not easy to come by. It was all very different to life in India, with a comfortable house and lots of servants. They missed the close friends they had had there and in Europe. Also my mother had not been well in Canada. Early in 1914, after a good deal of thought, they conclud ed that the Canada experiment had been a mistake. They let the ranch for a three-year term and returned to England. On reaching London my father rented a house near Kensington Gardens while they were considering where to live.

In the meantime we children had to start our education. It was decided that a French governess should be employed to look after us and teach us. We were then 6 years old and a considerable handful. In Canada we had led a wonderfully free life and by English standards our discipline was only moderate! We did not enjoy walks in the park nor the frequent visits to museums. The first two governesses found us more than they could manage. Eventually Miss Hayes, an experienced English governess, was engaged. She was splendid. She kept us in order, but we were devoted to her. She taught us extremely well and by the time we went to school we were both above the level of our age group.

London, before the First War, was full of interest for us children. The short stops in London, during our journeys to and from India and Canada, were quite different to living there. Everything was new and exciting, but our household was entirely a woman's world and it was decided that I should go to a boarding school as soon as I was seven and a half. A Catholic private school, where my Coats cousins had been, was selected. It was at Ladycross in Sussex and was called Ropers. And so, at the beginning of the summer term in 1915, I set off for school.

As soon as we had got back from Canada in 1914, war seeming certain, my father offered his services to the War Office. Soon after the War broke out Lord Kitchener became Secretary of State for War and put his great energies towards the formation of what became known as 'Kitchener's Army'. It was to be composed entirely of Volunteers and my father was one of its first Brigade Commanders.

Thanks to Miss Hayes, I found myself, when I went to school, well ahead in the work. As a result I did little and soon dropped back. Unfortunately for me, because my father was away, I had not been briefed in the customs of a school. For example I did not know that a master should be called 'Sir'. On the first morning I was called to the desk and given a smart smack on the cheek. I had no idea what it was for and quickly received another. However, I soon learnt and settled down well at Ropers.

One hears a lot about bullying, but I don't recall any at Ropers, nor later at Downside. I enjoyed my time at school, particularly the games. After my first year, I was promoted from soccer to rugger, which was a great advantage when I went on to Downside.

About a year after I went to Ropers my sister Angela went to school at Roehampton. We were close twins and she had not enjoyed being left alone with Miss Hayes during termtime.

During 1915 my father was appointed Deputy Adjutant and Quartermaster-General of the newly formed IX Corps, which was to take part in the Gallipoli Campaign. His Staff experience well qualified him for the appointment, but he was sad to leave his 55th Brigade, which he had looked forward to leading in France. However, it was War Office policy to send to France only younger men as Brigade Commanders. My father was 57 at the time and it came as a bitter blow to him. The 55th Brigade had been his baby. He had received the men as raw recruits and, with few officers or NCOs, he had trained them to become an efficient fighting formation of which he was proud. When they went to France he was to receive glowing reports of their achievements which gave him great pleasure.

In 1917 I moved from Ropers to Downside, a Catholic public school with an excellent Junior School, where I was very happy. It was run by Benedictine monks but half the teaching staff were lay masters. I made good progress at Rugger and got into the appropriate teams as I advanced up the school. I ended with three years in the 1st XV.

Except for my first year, Father Trafford, later Abbot Trafford, was Headmaster. He was a very remarkable character, a strict disciplinarian but respected and liked by the boys. He virtually ran the school.

Father Trafford gave up teaching when he became Headmaster, but he kept a finger in every pie. He knew all the boys. It was a fearsome occasion to be sent to him by a master and sometimes involved a punishment that hurt a great deal. Bathing would be forbidden after such a visit as we bathed without clothes in the swimming pool and the marks would be very apparent! Apart from unpleasant visits to the Headmaster, he would send for boys at random or call them into his room when they were asking for what was known as a 'long sleep'. This meant that one did not have to get up for early Mass. A long queue would form outside his room in the evening. If a boy had not asked for a long sleep for some time, he would sit him down in an armchair in his study and talk to him. It was an informal chat and enjoyed by the boys. In this way he got to know every boy in the school.

The Officers' Training Corps was another favourite of the Headmaster. The school employed a retired regular officer to run the Corps and to help him a splendid Foot Guards Sergeant-Major, who had afterwards been a 'Beefeater'. In spite of this high-powered staff, the Headmaster could not resist coming on parade himself and inspecting us. If his eagle eye lighted on a dirty button, it would be 'Up to my room, boy!'

My father, after his period with 9th Corps, was appointed to Salonika as Base Commandant in the rank of Major-General. That theatre was in the process of being developed and he found the job most interesting. Before long the problem of age caught up with him once more. He was now 58, was posted home and felt lucky to obtain an appointment with a District on the Lines of Communication in France. He was, therefore, abroad when the question arose of what I was likely to want to do and my school work be adjusted accordingly. The Headmaster had no doubt it should be the Army. This seemed natural and the Headmaster's proposal was accepted. Accordingly, I was put in the Army Class, which involved an emphasis on physics, chemistry and maths. I have always regretted the physics and chemistry at the expense of English and the Classics.

As one advanced in the school, life became more and more interesting. I much enjoyed it when I became a School Prefect and head of my house. At that time there were no housemasters. The Headmaster dealt directly with the School Prefects. The Head of the school had a very nice large room in the same passage as the Headmaster and we used to congregate there in the evenings. The Headmaster would come in and talk, and often used to ask us into his room to play bridge. And so my last term at school passed very pleasantly.

Now came the time for the Army Exam. The most important part of this was what was called 'Interview and Record'. The Headmaster would do his stuff on 'Record', the rest was up to me. But the Headmaster was not one to leave anything to chance. He had done his bit and now he briefed me in the greatest detail, even to the extent of telling me I must go to Trumper's in Curzon Street to get my hair cut. All passed off well and a letter arrived to say that I had been nominated for Sandhurst. I was to report early in January, 1926, as a Gentleman Cadet. In those days the parents paid for their sons to go to Sandhurst. Now the cadet is paid as a soldier.

I have always been grateful to Downside and more particularly to Father Trafford. Both my sons went to Downside in their turn.

CHAPTER II

Sandhurst

Whether or not we were called 'Mr Poett-Sir', we soon learnt our position. We were in the hands of a very excellent team of Brigade of Guards Sergeant-Majors. The smallest error in movement or dress would bring forth a roar! In fact, apart from being an extremely efficient lot, they were basically kindly.

On our first parade as 'Juniors' all of us had to shout out the name of the Regiment we wished to join. The Regimental representatives then got hold of us to see whether they thought we would fit in. We were all still in plain clothes, so there was a period of measuring and fitting for the many uniforms required. The periods allowed between activities were extremely short and all movement had to be done at the double or on bicycles. The bicycle was an essential part of our equipment and there was even a drill for bicycle parade.

We soon got into the routine. There was an immense amount of cleaning and polishing in our lives. The standard was perfection. I was in the old buildings and had a big double room to myself. All Gentleman Cadets, as we were called, had college servants who cleaned our rooms and made our beds. For a 'consideration' they would also help with polishing our belts, boots and riding gaiters.

Games were a most important feature of our lives. Soon after our arrival, I played in a trial for the R.M.C. rugger team. Unfortunately I received a heavy tackle and badly damaged the cartilage of my knee. This injury affected the rest of my time at Sandhurst and indeed hampered me permanently. I was not allowed to play any more rugger. Fortunately I had played goal in the Downside hockey team, was lucky to get into the R.M.C. hockey XI straight away and soon got my 'Blue'. The ban on playing rugger was a blow, as that was my main enjoyment. I was, however, continuing to have a lot of trouble with my knee. I could not kneel down as required on some weapon training exercises and there were other snags.

During the Summer term my knee got very bad and it was decided that an operation was necessary. I was sent to the Cambridge Hospital at Aldershot and all was ready for the operation when Sister Agnes of Boer War fame got to hear of it through an aunt of mine who was a close friend. In those days the Cambridge Hospital did not have the high reputation it has today. Sister Agnes got in touch with my parents and, with their agreement, she took charge. She was a pretty powerful lady! She rang the Cambridge Hospital and said that I was to be sent to her hospital, King Edward VII Hospital for Officers, in London, immediately in a taxi. The Cambridge Hospital was furious and the Sandhurst Authorities not pleased. Sister Agnes would not give way — she was very determined — and in no time I was speeding for London.

My family had taken a house at St Briac in Brittany for the summer. They had my sister Angela with them and could not change their plans, but Sister Agnes had taken charge! She had selected Mr Elmsley to do the operation. Unfortunately Elmsley was away and he could not do the operation at once. This meant that by the time he could manage it, Sister Agnes' Hospital would be closed for the summer holiday, during which she always went to Balmoral to stay with the Royal Family. So she arranged for the operation to be done at another nursing home. In the meantime, I stayed on at Sister Agnes' and was allowed freedom to go where I liked. In those days the nursing home was at 17 Grosvenor Crescent and Sister Agnes's house was next door, at number 16. She lived there in considerable style, with a butler, footmen and so on. She gave pleasant dinner parties, to one of which I was invited. She seemed to know everyone in London.

The time came for my operation and Sister Agnes attended it. The nursing home was a very different affair to 17 Grosvenor Crescent, where all the nurses seemed, to a boy of 18, well into middle age and wore dark dresses, whereas the nurses in the nursing home were young and attractive. When Sister Agnes came to see me the day after the operation she teased me about the good-looking nurses. She was wonderfully kind to me.

When I left the nursing home I went to Sussex to stay with my aunt and went to the nearest hospital for massage. It turned out that the operation had not been a complete success.

I went back to Sandhurst at the end of the summer break. I had missed a lot of the work and still had to be excused a good deal of the more strenuous activities. Altogether, that hard rugger tackle had greatly interfered with my time at Sandhurst.

The time now came for me to settle, finally, the Regiment for which I wished to apply. The Dorsetshire Regiment would have been a natural for me. I was very fond, however, of anything to do with horses and the Durham Light Infantry appealed to me very much. It was more than twenty years since my father had commanded the Dorsetshire Regiment and he had lost touch. The D.L.I had a tremendous polo reputation and he was happy for me to apply for them.

Now my final term at Sandhurst was coming to an end. I soon heard that I had been successful in getting the D.L.I. vacancy and that I would be gazetted to the regiment on 1 September, 1927. The Passing-Out Parade followed and then a big dinner in London with friends.

Sandhurst was over and I had enjoyed it.

CHAPTER III

The Durham Light Infantry

Soon after leaving Sandhurst, I received my joining instructions from the War Office. I was to join the 1st Battalion the Durham Light Infantry at Southampton and embark with them for Egypt in November, 1927. This was splendid news. We would be stationed at Alexandria; it was a single-battalion station and a popular one. The rest of the British Troops, Egypt (B.T.E.), as the army in Egypt was called, were split between Cairo and the Canal Zone.

I now had two months' leave to get myself ready. The Regiment sent me lists of the uniform and other kit I would require and the names of the regimental tailors. My father chose Hawkes which had been his tailor. Then followed fittings for uniform and plain clothes, plus a great deal of advice from my father's army friends in Bath! My family had bought Filleigh House on Bathwick Hill a few years before I went to Sandhurst.

All went well with the preparations, except, probably, the large bills that resulted. I was given a very fine Purdey gun and then, at the suggestion of my new Commanding Officer, a saddle, so when I set off to join my Regiment at Southampton, I was grateful and happy.

We were to sail on the Hired Transport *City of Marseilles*. It was not up to usual 'trooper' standard but was an ideal way of getting to know people in the Regiment; also to learn more about the Regiment and what should or should not be done.

The routine on board was designed to keep everyone as busy as possible. P.T. featured daily and there were lectures about Egypt and a variety of other subjects. There were daily parades and inspections and as much drill as the deck space allowed. I shared a cabin with an officer called Richardson, a very nice man and an excellent officer. I learnt a lot from him. I had been allotted a platoon and the voyage was an ideal chance to get to know them. They were about my age and friendly. Almost all of them were Geordies from Tyneside. None had been abroad before and it was all a great excitement for them.

Their accommodation below decks was terrible. They slept in hammocks hung in the small spaces allotted. One of the jobs of a subaltern was to visit the entire ship every hour and check on the sentries who were placed at intervals, as a protection against fire. The job of visiting was split up into four-hour periods. It was not pleasant, particularly at night and in rough weather. The atmosphere was extremely thick and squeezing between the hammocks difficult. Midnight to 4am was a particularly unpopular time.

And so the journey passed – now into the Mediterranean and an improvement in the weather – and then Alexandria. We steamed into the harbour but were not to disembark until the next morning.

Alexandria was a large city, a mixture of new and old, of Europe and the East, the old Native quarter with its bazaars, each dedicated to a different trade, merging into the European quarter with its wide, tree-lined streets and modern buildings and shops. It was an important centre for trade in the Eastern Mediterranean with a mixed population of Europeans, Egyptians, Arabs and Levantines. Most had business interests in cotton and other products of the East.

The Regiment was to be quartered at Mustapha Barracks which were on the outskirts of the city on the seashore. It comprised a large number of wooden huts, close to the beach, and some two-storied buildings. These larger buildings contained the offices, quartermasters' stores and other administrative functions. The Officers' Mess and our living quarters were two-storied buildings close to the Mess. Our rooms were comfortable and airy with plenty of bathrooms. There was a 600-yard rifle range in the barrack area, firing out to sea. The accommodation huts surrounded a tarmac parade ground. Altogether it was a pleasant and convenient set-up. One could put on bathing trunks in one's quarter and walk down to the beach.

The stables and the transport lines were at the opposite end of the barracks to the rifle range. One of the first things that the Regiment did after our arrival was to plan for the polo season which would start in the following Spring. Both the D.L.I. battalions had polo clubs, with valuable polo funds. The system was for the club to loan an officer a certain percentage of the cost of an approved pony. It was, if I remember, an interest-free loan. At any particularly important tournament the officer taking the loan was expected to allow the pony to be used by any member of the team. A lot of help was given by the experienced players to young officers in choosing and purchasing a pony. The Commanding Officer, Colonel Claude Matthews, had been a member of de Lisle's famous team which had won the Inter-Regimental tournament three years running against all the best Cavalry regiments in India. His help and advice was, therefore, invaluable to us.

There was a splendid system, in the days of horsed cavalry, by which during the 'Individual Training Season' the troop horses were loaned to infantry regiments for the cost of the insurance. In Egypt at that time the cost was 10 shillings a month! We were able to keep these horses for the whole of the winter and I was lucky enough to be allotted one. It had been well schooled in its Regiment, The Royals, and would make a good polo pony. Colonel Matthews had a good liaison with the Colonel of the Royals who saw that we had good ponies. In addition, I bought, with the aid of the Polo Club and a lot of advice, an excellent Arab pony which I kept for the rest of my time in Egypt. I was now well set up to start polo.

My other main sporting activity at Alexandria was rugger. The Battalion had a strong side and I was lucky enough to get a place in it. I had always been enthusiastic since my days at Downside, but had not been allowed to play while at Sandhurst because of my knee trouble. Our Medical Officer at Alex assured me that if I continued to play I would end up with a stiff leg for the rest of my life! But I was not prepared to listen. I had had enough of that story at Sandhurst. When I was very fit — which I was — my knee, if well bound up, would swell a bit but then go down. I had an immense amount of fun out of rugger. There was an Inter-Regimental competition during the winter which we won. This involved going to Cairo almost every week. In addition I got into the 'Army in Egypt' team, and had a lot of excellent rugger with them.

Other sporting activities during the winter included duck shooting. We had acquired a lease for the Regiment of a splendid shoot on Lake Maryut. This was run by one of the Company Commanders, 'Dad' Heslop, who was himself a first-class shot. The lake was shot once a week and we took it in turns to have a gun. We would catch a local train from Alex at about 5am and get off at a station close to the lake. There we would be met by Egyptian 'boys'. Each of us would then get into a punt, in which we would be taken to our hides. These were often quite a distance along narrow creeks with the rushes almost meeting overhead. On either side there would be quacks as we went along. Our hides would be a barrel carefully camouflaged with reeds. The 'boy' would wait in the punt, under cover, ready to 'pick up' when the shoot was over. We kept quiet and still until day began to break. At the appropriate moment 'Dad' Heslop would fire a shot and the fun began. It seldom lasted much more than an hour and then the duck would cease to come back. For this short time it was tremendous. One morning, I remember, 'Dad' had fifty duck to his gun. And so home to breakfast, after a wonderful morning.

The winter passed. I worked hard at training for polo, schooling my ponies and schooling myself. There was a 'polo pit' where one sat on a wooden horse and hit the ball which would then roll back for another shot. I spent many hours in the polo pit, but even more schooling my ponies on the practice ground and hitting the ball there.

Then there was the social life of Alex. Many kind and very hospitable local people, cotton magnates and others, gave us young officers a wonderful time. It was not surprising that we found life in the Army pretty good! However, it was not only the sporting and social side that we enjoyed. The Battalion took soldiering seriously. Within the first week of arrival at Alex, I found myself on 'the square' with the recruits who had joined recently. The 'menu' was drill, weapon training and all the duties required of a private soldier, but with the requirement that I should do better than any of the others! This lasted about four weeks. In addition there was my Platoon to get to know and look after. There were only three officers in my company and so there were plenty of company duties to perform.

This shortage of officers existed throughout the Battalion and indeed the Army. I did not find the shortage of officers a disadvantage, as one gained responsibility early.

In the New Year we went to a camp in the Desert near the Giza pyramids, for 'Collective Training'. It was tough training, particularly on big exercises. The nights were exceedingly cold and the days were hot. Marching longish distances over rough ground was thirsty work and water was strictly rationed. It was all new to me and I enjoyed it. When a long exercise was over, we had a quieter day or two and we used to go to the Mena House Hotel, which would be full of friends.

Soon after our return from this training Colonel Matthews arranged for me to do a six-week attachment to The Royals and pass through their Riding School. It was a wonderful experience and I much enjoyed it. I did everything that a young cavalry officer or recruit did. I took part in 'stables' and grooming. I had sessions with the farrier and, under his supervision, made and put on a shoe. The Officers of the Regiment were very kind to me and made me feel completely at home in the Mess.

Then the polo season in Alex started and all the practice and work I had put in paid off. We ran three teams in the Regiment and played in a lot of local tournaments. At the end of the summer in Alex the time came to pick the Regimental team for the Infantry and Gunner tournament which took place in Cairo during the winter season. We had a peculiar system for choosing the team. All members of the Polo Club, in practice all the officers, had a vote and chose three members for the team and then those three chose the fourth. I was thrilled to find myself voted in as one of the team. This Inter-Regimental tournament involved the team going up to Cairo about once a week for the eliminating rounds. Our team consisted of the Colonel at No 1, Bobby Simpson at No 2, Jos Percy at No 3, and I was Back. We kept our ponies in Cairo until the Tournament known as the 'Gordon Cup' was over.

We worked our way through the Gordon Cup heats and reached the final. There we were up against the R.H.A. team, who were the favourites. When the gong went we were all square. This meant extra time. I forget the length of the extra time allowed, but it was split into two halves. The first team to score a goal was the winner. As the 'Back', when in the attack I would be lurking behind our forward players, but, if possible, within reach of the opponents' goal, waiting for a chance to come through. My chance came, a loose ball in my direction. I was able to reach it and it was safely between the posts!

Now it was back to Alex for the summer season. Soon my company went to Sidi Bisch to complete our annual weapon training. An officer was expected to end up as a 1st class shot with both the rifle and Lewis gun. There was always anxiety until the results came down the range. Fortunately all was well! Sidi Bisch was a delightful oasis running down to a sandy beach with an island about 100 yards out to sea. We had tents close to the sea shore and the bathing was perfect.

Then back to Alex for military training and other military duties. In the meantime polo and other sports were in full swing. The 12th Lancers had rented the Parsonage for the summer from the Church Authorities and kept their ponies with us. They were a great asset to our Alex polo. They produced a good side for all our tournaments and raised the level of our own polo. Apart from polo, there was sailing. We hired boats from the Alexandria Yacht Club on Sundays and would sail out to a nearby island and sun-bathe and swim.

My father died in December, 1929. My mother advised me not to return from Egypt as I could not arrive in time for the funeral. My eldest sister Phyllis had gone to Filleigh House to be with my mother.

Towards the end of 1929 the time came to choose the three elected members of the Regimental Polo Team. I was again elected. I bought another pony with the aid of the Polo Club. It was a large and strong country-bred grey, but it was not a success. I found it too much of a handful. My very handy Arab was much more my number, even though it was not so powerful at riding off an opponent. My Arab, like many others, had the nasty habit of biting when riding off. I muzzled it, but even that was not a full cure. On one unfortunate day I was 'riding off' the Colonel and my pony had a chunk out of his breeches! The Colonel pulled up and there were few things he didn't call me. At the end of the chukka he told me not to worry, but of course it was my fault for not having better control of my pony.

I think it must have been in January, 1930, that I heard that I would be posted to the 2nd Battalion in India during the spring. Much as I had enjoyed myself in Alex, India would be more exciting. The 2nd Battalion was about to move to Razmak, a frontier station in Waziristan. In that district the Army allowed no wives because an almost permanent state of war existed between the tribesmen and our forces. The route to Razmak lay through Bannu in the North-West Frontier Province and was only open on certain days of the week, when the heights on either side of the road were picketed with our troops to ensure safe passage. This was to give me my first taste of active service. The Battalion would be there for one year.

Colonel Matthews gave me a month's leave so that I could see my family before going to India. I was then to join the troopship at Port Said.

I left Alex towards the end of January on a Lloyd-Triestino ship bound for Venice. This involved missing the Regimental Polo Team and the Gordon Cup, but the thought of home leave followed by India made up for that. I was sorry to leave Alex; I had enjoyed my time there and learnt a lot.

The sea voyage to Venice in a comfortable liner was a pleasant experience. The next evening I set off by train for Paris, 2nd class and sitting up all the way. I stayed two days in Paris with my sister and then went to England and on to Filleigh House and a warm welcome from my mother.

The plan for my return was to cross the Channel by the Le Havre route so that I could have a full day in Paris with Phyllis and then take the train for Genoa, where I would pick up my Lloyd-Triestino for Port Said and there I would connect with the Trooper on which I would sail for India. These arrangements had been specially agreed by my Regiment at Alex because I had been in hospital. They broke down at the very first stage. I got into my berth on the cross-channel steamer and went to sleep expecting to be woken up in time for Le Havre. The steward came in at the appropriate time but with the disturbing information that we were still in port in England, held up by fog in the Channel. This was serious; if I missed the Trooper I would have to pay my way to India.

Phyllis fortunately knew of the fog and had reacted splendidly. She got a message to me at the boat that she would meet me at the station in Paris and would make all arrangements. The fog lifted and we were off and sure enough Phyllis was at the Gare du Nord. She hurried me across Paris to the station for Genoa. If I missed the boat there I could pick it up at Naples. I could have caught the boat at Genoa but chose to go on by train to Naples and spend a day in that lovely city. It had been a close thing but now all was well.

My baggage was waiting for me at Port Said and when the Trooper came in I embarked. I found there was a D.L.I. draft on board for the 2nd Battalion. Captain Philips was the Draft Conducting Officer. He was an experienced officer returning to India from leave and I would be his No 2 with the draft.

The voyage was uneventful but hot, the month being April.

17

The routine on board was much the same as I had experienced in the *City of Marseilles* but this was a regular Trooper and much more comfortable.

CHAPTER IV

The North-West Frontier

India was in sight and our boat edged into its place alongside the quay at Bombay. Now my first Indian journey began. It was an experience in itself. Philips had his own bearer and the Adjutant had engaged one for me. A bearer was an important figure in one's life. He went everywhere with you, on operations, on training, when travelling and so on. A good bearer made all the difference to one's comfort in India. Mine was good. He had been with another officer in the Regiment. He was loyal and honest and I kept him for the six years I was in India.

An essential item of equipment in India, and indeed in Egypt, was a bedding roll. This was taken on operations, on training and for travelling. It consisted of rolled-up blankets and pillows and often a canvas bath with a collapsible wooden frame. In addition we all had enamel basins with a canvas top to hold our washing things. The bedding roll would also take a change of clothing. The outer part of the roll was made of strong canvas held in shape by leather straps with a strong handle.

When travelling, an officer would have a sleeping compartment on the train. His bearer would be in another compartment with the servants and would attend at the door of his master's sleeper during any long train stops to guard it and in case anything was wanted. There would be stops for meals at a station restaurant and, if it was a troop train, the stop would be somewhere where the soldiers could have a meal. In the evening one's bearer would lay out the bedding roll ready for the night.

Our journey to Razmak would take about two weeks. It would, therefore, require several stops at a transit camp so that we could all have baths. The transit camps would also have facilities for football, P.T. and other military training. It was important that the men remained fit during this long journey.

On the day after our arrival at Bombay we set off for Razmak.

During the day I spent most of the time in Philips' compartment and learned a lot about India and the Razmak we were going to. The sight of an Indian railway station is an experience in itself. Every platform is packed tight with people sitting on or standing over their baggage. The trains were packed to capacity and the roofs of the coaches were equally crowded. It seemed the same thing at every station we passed.

It was April and the country was already getting a burnt-up look. Men and women were in the fields tending their crops and their livestock. The special respect in which cattle were held was easily seen. It was hot and the stops for food and to stretch one's legs and have the men's coaches cleaned were always welcomed. And so we went on, seemingly for ever. The first full-day stop was particularly enjoyed. If I remember we went for a route march and during the middle of the day we rested in hutted accommodation. During the route march there was something new to see all the time. In the evening there would be something like a 'kick-about' at football, perhaps 50 a side. Anything to provide exercise and change.

Then on we went. After the first few days it became a dull and tiring journey. Then we came to the end of the railway at Bannu — a foul spot, a real oven. There we must wait for a 'column' which would take us the 100 miles or so up the Tochi Pass to Razmak. The picketing of the heights bordering the route to protect the columns of lorries against tribesmen and snipers was a considerable operation undertaken by troops based at Bannu. It meant that the convoy of lorries — the columns — were limited to a very few days of the week. In the meantime officers and men were reasonably comfortably accommodated at Bannu. There was a Station Officers' Mess where we were well looked after, but to go outside at any time except the evening or early morning involved being hit by a really scorching sun. A number of visits had to be made each day to see that all was well with the soldiers and organize their activities.

Then the day came for the column to leave for Razmak; going up the Tochi Pass with the high hills on either side and our pickets on them was the first experience of many that were to follow.

While we were in Razmak that part of Waziristan was in a very disturbed state. The tribesmen of hostile villages frequently raided and burnt the villages of those which had come to terms with the 'Raj'. There were constant ambushes of convoys and sniping at patrols and the situation was developing into a state of war. In fact, before we left, the operations had developed to a state when they were recognized for the award of the General Service medal.

Razmak was an important outpost on the frontier. The camp was entirely surrounded by wire and other defences, with observation towers which included machine-gun and mortar emplacements. The entrance to the camp was strongly defended and entry or exit after dark was forbidden. The garrison consisted of a brigade, which always included a British battalion; in addition there were mountain gunners, a squadron of Sappers and Miners and other supporting units.

The sports grounds and a small airfield were outside the camp perimeter. Although the airfield had a slight slope, we were able to play polo on it, for which we used the Indian Army Service Corps ponies. The airfield was rough ground but it served our purpose. We had not brought any of our Regimental ponies to Razmak, having left them to be looked after by an Indian Cavalry regiment at Sialkot, the Battalion's last station in the plains. At that time a lot of ponies were bought in and then sold to us on arrival in India. These Australian ponies, known as 'Walers', were bigger and stronger than the country-breds. They would arrive only half-trained, but while we were at Razmak they would be schooled by Indian Cavalry Warrant Officers and N.C.O.s. They made an excellent job of it. There was a draw among officers wishing to purchase. None of us had seen the ponies so it was something of a gamble. I was lucky and drew a good one which I kept for the rest of my time in India.

This was the Razmak into which Philips and I, with our convoy, drove in April, 1930.

A British battalion at Razmak was kept at full strength in officers and men and the Officers' Mess was, therefore, always a pleasant place. In the evenings many of us would play Bridge. There were usually three tables. The Mess stakes were small and no other card game was allowed.

The Commanding Officer was Colonel Robin Turner, popularly known as the 'little man'. He was a bachelor and was always addressed as 'Colonel'. It was the custom to call all other officers by their Christian names.

I was posted to 'A' Company, which was commanded by Oswald Paget. He had known my family in Dorset when he was a boy and my sisters only a little older.

There was not much time to settle in, as the Battalion was about to go on 'column'. Although this 'column' was to show the flag and had no punitive purpose, the Battalion went out fully operational with exactly the same precautions and drill as though we were expecting hostile action from the tribesmen. In fact, any relaxation from the strict 'column' discipline would have been likely to provoke action. The tribesmen were always on the lookout for lapses.

The 'column' drill required one to be extremely fit. I was reasonably fit but not as fit as I soon became and I remember finding that first 'column' very hard going.

The 'column' would form up inside the camp perimeter. An 'advanced guard' would lead and the 'advanced guard' commander would control the speed of the convoy and the placing of the pickets. Next came the picketing troops; their assignment was a really hard one. A picket could be a platoon or less, seldom more. The picketing troops, in total, might consist of a company. As each picket was called forward in turn, the hilltop which the commander was required to occupy and hold would be pointed out to the picket commander. He would then lead his picket at the double up a spur towards it. About 50 yards from the top he would gather his men and then rush the top. It was the last 20 yards or so that were the most dangerous. If the hill was occupied by hostile tribesmen it was then that they would open fire. Safely at the top, the commander would put out a special flag to show that the hill was occupied. When the advanced guard commander was satisfied that the route was safely picketed, he and the rest of the column would move on.

Behind the picketing troops would come the main body of the battalion, the gunners, and the transport and supplies. In this column the transport was all pack animals, camels, mules and ponies. Then would come the rearguard. One of the most important responsibilities of the rearguard was to make certain that all the pickets placed by the advanced guard were called in and were safely down before the column moved on. The picket flags were an important part of this procedure, but there were other safeguards as well.

One hard feature of a 'column' was thirst. Movement, both marching and climbing, was thirsty work, but the amount of water that could be carried on pack animals was very limited and strict water discipline had to be maintained. We started a day with a full water bottle but no drinking was allowed without the permission of an officer and this would not normally be given until arrival at the night's camp.

I used to find the withdrawal from a picket difficult. It had to be done at the double. Running down the steep rock-strewn slope of a frontier hill was tough on the best of knees and I found it quite a hazard. On reaching the level of the convoy, the men of the picket, led by its commander, would double through the column to the picketing troops in front and then become available to be sent up on another picket. On arrival at the camp site for the night there would be intense activity. A perimeter wall, made of stones, would be built and defensive positions prepared. While this was being done, defensive posts outside the perimeter would be occupied. Until the CO was satisfied with the defences, the longed-for meal would not be served.

I have spent time in describing the routine of a column because this formed such an important part of our lives. In fact, these columns were the purpose for which we were in Razmak.

As time passed during our stay in Razmak, the situation with the tribesmen became progressively worse. The events we were training for on columns did happen. We were fired on as we rushed the hilltops or as we galloped down to rejoin the convoy. The training paid off and we got exceedingly fit in the process. I don't believe I have ever been so physically fit as I was at Razmak.

Operational columns became more and more frequent and those for showing the flag gave way to others in which the civil authorities had to collect a fine or impose some penalty on a village. In between columns, we enjoyed the ordinary activities of the camp — competitive games with the other units, the rather elementary polo on the rough and sloping airfield and a major task which the Commanding Officer had set the Battalion for its year at Razmak — work on a new sports ground. The garrison was short of any good level ground and the C.O. decided that we should bequeath to the garrison a properly levelled ground. This would involve a great deal of earth-moving, which, in those days, would have to be done by hand, there being no mechanical earth-moving equipment available. Each company was given a task and we set about it.

During our time we had two visits of interest; one from the Viceroy, Lord Irwin, and another from the C in C, Lord Birdwood. Lord Birdwood had known my father well at Gallipoli and when he came to me in the line of officers to be introduced, he asked whether I was any relation. It was nice to be able to tell him that I was his son.

The time passed quickly in Razmak and before long we found ourselves preparing for the move to our new station, Barrackpore, some 15 miles from Calcutta. One day the C.O. called me to his office and told me that the Governor of Bengal had asked the Regiment to provide him with an ADC for six weeks at Christmas when Calcutta was very busy with social events. He said he would like to send in my name, if I agreed. I was delighted but had to await developments.

Eventually the time came for the Battalion to leave Razmak. It had been a strenuous time but an interesting experience. The journey to Barrackpore was not unlike the journey from Bombay, except that travelling with the whole Regiment in special troop trains for a single destination was quicker and easier. As far as I can remember the journey was completed in one week.

1 My parents about 1890

2 "The drive through Manipur was fascinating . . . . They were very small and backward people carrying spears and blowpipes." (p.30)

3 After the water jump (see p.55). *Left to right,* Senior Instructor, Group Captain Newnham, Brigadier Hugh Kindersley, the author.

4 "King George VI and the Queen . . . . came round the whole Division" (p.56). The author is on the right, standing behind the King.

CHAPTER V

Barrackpore

Eventually, after the long journey across India, we reached Barrackpore. En route we had passed through the centre of the Punjab, including Lahore, then the United Provinces and Delhi, on into Bihar and so to Calcutta. In fact, we had had a glimpse from the train windows of some of the most important and interesting parts of India. Then from Calcutta, 15 miles north, to the small siding at Barrackpore. Here we met up with the Regimental families. The men had been separated from their wives for the best part of a year. Some, whose wives had remained at Sialkot, had been able to take leave, but during the latter part of our time at Razmak operations had made leave difficult to get.

At Barrackpore the men were accommodated in two-storied barrack blocks. There were married quarters for the soldiers' families, but there was only a small establishment of married soldiers allowed. The officers rented their own houses - known always as bungalows - according to how much they could afford. Officers aged 26 and over drew a marriage allowance. Officers below that age were known as 'living in sin'. They drew no allowances. The unmarried officers lived in a block of officers' quarters some little way from the mess. We each had a large single room with a high ceiling and a bathroom attached. The bathroom had running cold water, a wide concrete shelf for one's basin and a tin bath. In the hot and sticky climate of that part of India a bath was an important feature of life. When a bath was required one's bearer would summon the *beesti*, a low rank of servant, who had charge of all the bathroom arrangements and the 'thunderbox'. He would heat the water in large old-fashioned petrol cans and pour in the cold water to a suitable mixture. The bathroom door leading to the servants' quarters was always kept locked until the *beesti* was required to attend to fix either the bath or the thunderbox. Then the master would unlock the door and give a shout. I always found the tin bath quite comfortable. With one's feet on the concrete wall, one could lie down and soak.

The Officers' Mess, the quarters and the barrack block were spread over a considerable area and a bicycle was essential for getting about. The whole was contained in what was known as the cantonment. This also included the club and most of the houses belonging to business people or British officials. In Calcutta British businessmen were always referred to as 'box wallahs'. They used the same term speaking of each other.

Barrackpore was a pleasant suburb of Calcutta. It had good bungalows and gardens and a golf course. There was also a Government House, used by the Governor in summer. There was a shopping area, known as the Bazaar, and a race course with a polo ground in the middle, which we were soon using.

Every Sunday morning, we used to hold a Polo Pony Parade after church. This served as a way of entertaining the local people. It also gave a stimulus to the *syces* (grooms) to turn out their ponies well and give an extra smartening to the saddlery. A syce generally looked after two ponies. I soon bought a second pony, a country-bred to go with the 'Waler' I had bought while we were in Razmak. This involved a lot of work to get them up to standard for polo. The battalion usually had a before-breakfast parade of P.T. or something of the sort. Those schooling used the period for work on their ponies. I was always on the polo ground by 6 am.

Soon after our arrival at Barrackpore, I was invited to a tennis party at Government House, where the Governor had come for the weekend. It was obvious that I was to be vetted for the ADC job during the winter. I heard from Colonel Turner that I had been accepted and would start at the end of November and continue for six or seven weeks.

In the meantime, there was plenty to do. It was the 'hot weather' and one company was always in the 'Hills' at Lebong, close to Darjeeling, a night's journey in the train from Calcutta and then a change to narrow gauge through the Tea Gardens to the railhead at Lebong. The barracks looked over a small 'dirt' race course with a polo ground and sports fields in the middle. There was a wonderful view of the Himalayan range and particularly Kanchenjunga. Lebong was about 500 feet below Darjeeling. During the summer months, the principal offices of the Government of Bengal moved to Darjeeling and there was a Government

House there. The Military HQ also moved to Darjeeling. No cars were allowed except those belonging to the Governor. The means of getting around was by rickshaw.

Meanwhile in the Plains it was the leave season. Everyone in theory had the chance of 'Home Leave', for eight months, every three years. This allowed two months for the journey and six months at home. All those not taking home leave were entitled to two months' 'Privilege' leave. The Battalion was, therefore, very short of officers during that period and a young subaltern would find himself in command of a company, sometimes two companies, during most of the summer. This meant a busy life, excellent experience but no extra pay! The most important thing during this long, hot and sticky summer was to keep the soldiers occupied and happy. The monsoon generally broke towards the end of June and that brought a drop in temperature but disadvantages as well.

I decided to learn Urdu during the summer months. Every British battalion had an Indian Platoon which looked after the mules of the Machine Gun Company. It was obviously an advantage to be able to communicate with them and other Indians. Also one got a grant if one passed an exam and I rather think there was a little extra pay for those who had qualified. I had an excellent *munshi* (teacher) and I was lucky enough to pass.

In November I went to Government House. There were three permanent ADCs. They made me welcome and taught me the ropes. I was given the acting rank of Captain so that I was on the same footing as the others and then I was fitted into the roster. The duties were taken strictly in turn. The ADC-in-waiting would spend his day in attendance with the Governor. This would involve, first, riding with HE before breakfast. The usual routine was to make for the Race Course, crossing the Maidan, a large park-like area between Government House and the Race Course, then two or three circuits of the tan track which ran round the inside of the course and then home. After breakfast one would spend the morning in the Governor's outer office receiving visitors and showing them in when the Governor was ready. One would accompany HE on any outside engagements he might have or for a lunch. Much the same routine in the afternoon.

The Governor was Sir Stanley Jackson. He had been a very well-known cricketer and later an MP. He was very pleasant company with many interests and a keen sportsman. Lady Jackson was also delightful. The ADC next in-waiting would spend the day with her in much the same way, starting with an early morning ride. I had brought my two polo ponies with me and my syce looked after them in the Government House stables. They were well behaved and no trouble with the Governor's horses. The next day, the responsibility would be looking after the guests' plans for the day, arrange cars and accompany them when desired.

The ADCs lived in a comfortable wing of Government House. We had our own sitting room and dining room and only had our meals with HE and Lady Jackson when we were on duty.

There would be a number of big functions each year, such as dinners for 100 guests. As he and Lady Jackson approached the guests, who would be assembled round the walls of the anteroom, one of the ADCs would be responsible for calling out the guests' names. It was a considerable task to know every guest by name. There would be hurried consultations between the ADCs before the arrival of HE to check on names.

When in uniform the ADCs wore frock coats and a stock of these were kept at Government House and loaned to ADCs. In plain clothes there were certain functions for which a morning coat was worn; fortunately I had mine with me. The only thing I had to buy was a grey top hat. I still have the one that I bought in Calcutta.

And so a very enjoyable break from ordinary soldiering came to an end. I had learned a little about how the Government of India functioned and I had met a great many interesting people.

CHAPTER VI

ADC to General Bethell

My Battalion was now in the midst of the training season. Company camps and battalion exercises were the order of the day. We had a good regimental football side and were expected to support our team by being present at matches. There was not much military competition but the local Indian clubs were good and matches in Calcutta were hard-fought affairs. Apart from polo, my own sports activities mainly centred on rugger. We had a good rugger side but the best of the rugger in India were the 'inter-provincial' matches, Bengal, Bombay, and Madras taking part. I was lucky enough to get into the Bengal side when in Calcutta and Bombay when we were there.

While I was at Government House I had met the General Commanding the Presidency and Assam District, General H.K. Bethell, known as 'The Beetle'. He had distinguished himself during the First War as a very young brigade commander. He asked my Colonel whether I might deputize for his permanent ADC while he was on home leave. My Colonel was not keen on my becoming an ADC again, but it was difficult for him to refuse the General and it was agreed.

This was a very different job to the previous one. The General was a tough character and I worked extremely hard and learned a great deal. It was a 6am to midnight job. The General's house was at Fort William in Calcutta.

The day started with exercising the ponies. The General had four and I had two. We would make for the tan track round the Race Course with the string of syces riding the other ponies behind us. We would then ride each pony in turn. After being with the General for about a week, I knew exactly how he liked the exercising done, and as he was always very busy I would often do it all myself.

After breakfast the General might visit a unit, in which case I would go with him, or he might have interviews or office work to attend to; a certain amount of the office work would spill on to me. The General certainly saw that I was kept busy.

During the time I was with him, the General did a number of tours. The Indian Railways would provide a special coach containing a sitting room, dining room and two or three sleeping compartments. The servants would be accommodated elsewhere in the train. This coach would be attached to whatever train was needed or put in a siding and would become our base for a few days. The arrangements for this coach involved a good deal of work with the Railways and the District HQ staff. When the General had decided with his senior staff officer, the GS01, what he wanted to do, the details would be worked out between the staff and me. With so many people involved, very careful checking was necessary to ensure that the coach would be in the right place to meet the right people. There was no margin of error.

One long trip started in the coach at Calcutta. From there we went to Silchar, the HQ of the Assam Valley Light Horse who were to be inspected, then up to Shillong, to stay with the Governor of Assam. A Gurkha Battalion stationed there was to be seen the next morning on an exercise. The exercise was to start with a long night march. Towards the end of dinner at Government House the General said to me that it would be a good idea if I did the march with the Battalion and could tell him in the morning how it had gone! I changed at speed into my khaki drill and was off to Battalion HQ. Fortunately I was very fit and could manage the long march across country in the dark. The General had done this to test me out and he required a full report in the morning.

After Shillong we went through Manipur State to Imphal, which became famous during the Second World War as the battle in which the Japanese advance into India was stopped. The drive through Manipur was fascinating. The road was very narrow and we kept meeting groups of Manipuri. They were very small and backward people carrying spears and blowpipes. They were friendly but frightened of us. The road through the hills was narrow and twisty and neither the General nor I had much confidence in our driver. After once nearly going over the side, I was made to drive. I doubt that I was any safer, but we did arrive safely at Imphal!

At Imphal we were looked after by the High Commissioner and

the political situation in Manipur was discussed; also, equally important, the arrangements for the duck shoot the next day and the polo the following day. Before anything else, however, the time had come for the General's official call on the Maharaja. I went with him. The Maharaja was very agreeable and told us that he would be lending us ponies for the polo match.

The duck shoot the next day was tremendous. I have never seen anything like the quantity of duck. As usual we were in our hides on the lake before dawn, with a boy in a boat to pick up. Then, at first light, the shooting started. Duck came on and on for three or four hours, in undiminished numbers, before gradually lessening. After two hours or so I was exhausted and had a bad headache, getting worse as the morning wore on. I have no idea what the total bag was was, nor how many duck I collected myself; it must have been a good number, but I did not really enjoy it.

The next afternoon there was to be a polo match between two local sides. We were fitted into one of them. Imphal is one of the places which claims to be where polo started. There are several other claimants. The local ponies were small and the sticks we used very long, probably 60 inches or more. In India at that time we were accustomed to playing with a stick of perhaps 49 to 51 inches. The technique at Imphal was to lean well out from the pony and strike the ball quite far from the pony. Both the General and I found it difficult, but our fellow players helped us as much as they could. It was quite an experience.

Our next stop was to visit a Post in the extreme north-east corner of India, Sadia, on the River Brahmaputra. We were the guests of a tea planter with a large group of estates near Dibrugath, close to the Brahmaputra River. He lived in considerable style and entertained us lavishly.

When the time came to leave, our host offered to take the General to a ferry point further down the river so that he could see more of his estates and the countryside. General Bethell gladly accepted. It was decided that I should join the boat as originally arranged, taking with me our considerable amount of baggage. My route from the tea planter's house to the ferry embarkation point was little more than a track, but the planter was quite convinced that the lorry he would lend me would easily make it. The distance to the ferry point was about 50 miles. In that part of India rain storms can be sudden and heavy. We were unlucky. When we were about half-way an exceptionally heavy storm hit us.

Soon the track became quite impassable. The more we pushed and pulled, the more firmly the wheels of the lorry dug in and the track gave way.

I had with me the General's uniform for a parade the next day and I had to reach him. I succeeded in getting a bullock cart from a village close by, moved all our kit into it and then set off again. With a good deal more shoving and pushing we eventually reached the ferry embarkation point, only to see the boat sailing away downstream. The only thing to do was to get back to the planter's house as quickly as possible and try to borrow another truck.

I was lent one, and we set off, this time down the good road taken by the General that morning. By now it was dark, but all went well. We reached the ferry point where the General's boat was still anchored in the river. I got all our kit into a small boat and went alongside.

It was now about 3am. The General was astonished and delighted to see me. He had been kept in touch with my day's adventures and had been assured that there was no chance of me or his uniform reaching him.

My first tour with General Bethell was over and we were now returning to Fort William, the District Headquarters in Calcutta, where the General had a number of local engagements, as well as office work to catch up on. But General Bethell was never quiet for very long. His mind was constantly active and his body had to follow suit.

We hadn't been back for more than a few days when he sent for me and said that he wanted to give a party for about 100 people. Would I produce a list 'by tomorrow' and we should then go through it together? It sounded quite simple but it was not. As a temporary ADC, I didn't know many of the local people, civil, official or military. There was, of course, the Calling Book, but a lot of research was involved in consulting the senior members of the staff and seeking their views on who should be asked. There were invitations to have printed, written on and addressed. The organization, the drinks and the eats would have to be faultless. A lot of burning of the midnight oil was ahead. I produced my list, which was added to by the General until the numbers were well over 100. Then I got down to it in a big way. As the General did not have a wife, the details of the party would have been handled by the ADC's wife, who was much liked by every one, but she was also away. The Flagstaff House servants were excellent and, once the orders were given, I didn't have to worry.

A week or so later we were both asked to stay with the Stanley Jacksons at Government House at Barrackpore. A few days off duty was what I wanted. The General stayed in the House and I was in a comfortable bungalow in the grounds. It was delightfully peaceful.

My next experience with the General was a week's pig-sticking in Bengal. The General had been invited by Calcutta Light Horse friends and he arranged for me to come with him. I had never done any pig-sticking. We were to use the Bengal short spear which is a good deal shorter than the Meerut spear. In Meerut and the Central Provinces, the aim is to secure 'first blood'. The spear is held in the same way as a lance and the boar is taken from behind. In Bengal the short spear was held in the middle and the rider would try to get level with the boar and strike down through the shoulders. At the speed one was going and with a very sharp spear, no force was required to penetrate deeply and kill or stop the pig. It was extremely exciting and care had to be taken to prevent the pig turning on the horse. A pig would suddenly appear out of the bushes and the chase would start.

During the week we stayed at what was known as a Dak Bungalow. These bungalows were to be found all over India. They were intended, in the first place, for Indian Civil Service officials on tour in their districts. When not required for officials, they were available for others. The occupant would pay a modest sum and bring with him his own servants, his bedding and food.

There were perhaps fewer boar than we had hoped for, but enough to keep everyone fully on the alert. My recollection is that we took it in turn to be in the lead and, therefore, have the first chance when a pig broke. In due course, on one of my turns, a pig went away and I had a marvellous chase eventually getting level and making a good 'spear'. Following a boar one did not attempt to guide the pony with the bit. One rode on a loose rein with perhaps a touch of the rein on the neck or using a bit of leg to bring the pony close into the boar. There were plenty of holes of various sorts in the ground being ridden over, but the pony was better able to avoid them without the aid of the rider. Towards the end of the week I took a bad fall. My pony put its foot into a hole and turned a somersault. I was lucky to escape with a damaged shoulder and nothing worse.

My final trip with the General was to the Sunderbans, the mass of small rivers and islands that make up the mouth of the Ganges. A boat was arranged which comfortably held the General's party of five or six guests. These included the Assistant Commissioner, who perhaps added some respectability to the trip, as he was glad to have the chance to visit a part of his territory not easily reached. We were told that there was an off-chance of having a shot at a tiger, so we all came suitably prepared. We landed on many of the little islands and saw a few of the primitive native villages. We did see, on one island, pug marks of tiger but no tiger had been reported. I had a long-distance shot at a crocodile with my .275 Mannlicher. The crocodile was basking on the sand at the water's edge some four or five hundred yards away. It gave a large jump in the air and seemed to fall back into the water. I had an audience of two or three while taking the shot and they were convinced it was a hit. I was less convinced, as it was a long shot and it could only have been a fluke to secure a kill. We set off in a ship's boat to have a look, but found nothing.

Towards the end of the trip we had something of a scare over a cypher telegram. There were a few points on the route where we stopped to pick up mail. The cypher was delivered in this way. It would be my job to decipher it. The General thought it might be something important requiring his return. He was anxious for a quick bit of work on my part. Our cypher book was in a sealed envelope and when I opened it I saw that the book was a practice one and not the real thing. I was horrified, but decided to go ahead with the decyphering and see what happened. I found at once that the decyphered telegram was making sense. Colonel Woods, the GS01 who had the key of the safe concerned, had discovered that the cypher book that I should have had was still in the safe and that I had been given a practice one. He acted accordingly and I was able to read his message. There was a certain amount of disorder in Bengal at that time, but there was no reason for the General to return early. We accordingly finished our voyage.

So ended my time with General Bethell for that year. I had got on well with him and he wrote a nice letter to my Colonel.

And so back to regimental soldiering at Barrackpore. There was the tail end of the summer ahead and I expect I went up to the hills with my company, but I forget when. I now knew that I would definitely be going to Government House for the next Christmas period and could look forward to that.

My second year at Government House proved even more enjoyable than the previous one. Sir Stanley and Lady Jackson were as kind as ever and the Staff were very welcoming. The Christmas house party seemed rather bigger and included the C-in-C, Sir Philip Chetwode, and the Naval C-in-C East Indies. Also Air Chief Marshal Sir Geoffrey Salmond, Sir Victor Sassoon and others.

This time there was to be a New Year Ball. The Stanley Jacksons decided that the ball would be opened by a set-piece 'Lancers' danced by the principal guests. Very few people knew how to do it and so there was a rehearsal on the previous day. The Governor and Lady Jackson did not take part in the rehearsal, I was detailed to deputize for the Governor and another ADC for Lady Jackson.

The high spot of the period was the Races, at which the Viceroy drove down the course in state; also the final of the Indian Polo Association tournament.

The festivities of the Calcutta season came to an end and I was again back on regimental duty. The few months either side of the New Year generally bring a spell of good weather and everything tended to get crowded into that period, both work and sport. It was then that the local polo tournaments sprang up all over India and we generally sent a team to Meerut and Bareilly.

My turn for home leave was due the following year, so I decided not to apply for the two months' privilege leave which was the normal period. I saved my money for the journey to England and enjoyed the local activities. In those days there was no assistance financially over leave, which was, therefore, a very expensive matter. The train to Bombay was expensive and the boat to England much more so. A year's restraint was necessary! However, a bonus unexpectedly came my way. I had got on well with General Bethell and now there was to be a vacancy on his staff for rather more than four months as General Staff Officer 3rd Grade. He asked my Commanding Officer whether he might have me for the job.

This was a wonderful opportunity. Not only would I learn a lot, but I would gain financially. I would draw Indian Army rates of pay, plus staff pay. I had been living close to the margin with my considerable polo expenses. From the service point of view, I would get valuable experience. 'Strafer Gott', the General Staff Officer 2nd Grade, would be my immediate boss. I would share an office with him and pick up a lot. Strafer became a very distinguished General during the Second War and had been selected to command the 8th Army, but was killed in an air accident as he was about to take up his post and was replaced by Monty. He was in the 60th and extremely nice. The Chief of Staff (GS01, 1st Grade) was easy to get on with. I had seen a lot of him when I was the General's ADC.

The Headquarters and the Officers' Mess were on the outskirts of Darjeeling, to the north and about 500 feet higher. We had a wonderful view of Everest and the Himalayas. Although staff work was new to me, I had learnt a certain amount as an ADC, and, under Strafer's able guidance, I soon picked up the essentials of my job. My time at General Bethell's Headquarters, as well as being interesting, was useful to me for the future.

When I returned to my Battalion the hot weather was practically over. I did not go to Government House that winter. I had already been away enough and now concentrated on my regimental duties.

CHAPTER VII

Travel and Romance

After a spell of home leave in 1934 I arrived at Barrackpore to be told that I was to go on a machine-gun course at Ahmadnagar, near Poona. I knew very little about the Vickers MG and for the next few weeks was hard at it. Then I was off to the MG School. Another long journey across India. I have never enjoyed courses of instruction and the part of the course which I most enjoyed were the weekends. A party of about six of us hired a Royal Mail bus every Sunday and went into the country to shoot, my particular friends in the party being Guy Peyton, a friend from Sandhurst days, and Roger Wilbram, a Greenjacket. Sand grouse were our main quarry. The technique was to hide at watering places and take the birds as they came in, rather like duck shooting. When the sand grouse ceased to come in, we would go for pigeons. There were supposed to be wild pea fowl about but they were scarce.

Towards the end of the course I was asked by an Indian Army Officer who was going in the direction of Calcutta and had just purchased a second-hand car whether I would like to go with him as a co-driver and share the expenses. Although I was happy to share the driving, I know nothing about the inside of a motor car and reckoned that I would be pretty useless in a breakdown.

The distance of the drive would be close on 1500 miles. We were going to take the most direct route which meant that the roads, in many places, would be poor. We did not plan to go through any major towns but would spend the nights at Dak bungalows and would adjust our route with that in mind. Our proposed route took us through every sort of Indian country. We started with Ahmadnagar in the Deccan, then through hilly country, jungle and so on. We were in luck; we didn't have any serious breakdown that could not be cured with a spanner and my companion's skill, or with a little patience if our trouble was

37

overheating. The Dak bungalows were adequate and the Indian in charge could produce and cook our food. All considered, we had a pretty trouble-free journey and saw much of the Indian countryside and people.

Soon after I got back to Barrackpore, Colonel Turner told me that I was to be the next Adjutant. He was finishing his period of command and was to be succeeded by Colonel Congreve whom I had known in Egypt and had agreed to the appointment. I was thrilled. To become Adjutant is the ambition of every young officer. I was to take over from Jumbo Sanders when he had taken the privilege leave to which he was entitled and I would be gazetted to the appointment on 1 October, 1934.

I sat in the office with Jumbo for a bit before he went on leave and learnt a lot from him. He had been an excellent Adjutant.

At about this same time it was announced that the Battalion would move to Bombay in the autumn. Two companies would be detached and located at Deolali on the Deccan. The move of a battalion in India was quite a complicated affair. Not only was there a handover and takeover of the the barracks and any special equipment, but there were usually operational and Internal Security schemes to pass on. The Adjutant is responsible to the Commanding Officer for almost everything and he is kept pretty busy in the process.

All went well with the move and we settled down comfortably at Bombay and Deolali. The Bombay Barracks were close to the sea and had a private bathing beach. The sports facilities were also good. The polo was run by Captain C.T.I. Roark, one of the best players in India, on behalf of the Turf Club. He was very helpful to the young players.

Colonel Congreve agreed to my taking my privilege leave in the summer and I decided to go to Japan for two months. I set off in June on a Lloyd Triestino boat bound for Shanghai. After a few days there, I took a smaller boat for Nagasaki. From there I went directly to Beppu, which had been recommended to me by a Staff Officer at Bombay with a Japanese wife, as an interesting small place, typical of Japan and without tourists. I stayed in a small Japanese inn. It was spotlessly clean. No one spoke anything but Japanese and there were no other foreigners. I had to eat the Japanese food which I did not like, but when I was hungry I could eat it! There was a large communal bath and bathroom, both very clean. Although it was theoretically communal, not a soul came near it when I was washing. The only snag was that the water was much too hot. I could not possibly have got into it. I had to content myself with splashing the water over me. The Japanese were friendly and welcoming. When I moved on I decided it should be to a small but more mixed hotel on the Inland Sea, on an island which I think was called Miajima. It was a most beautiful spot and the food was more appetizing. Bathing was no problem. I took a rowing boat out from the hotel, anchored it and dived in.

My next stopping place was Kyoto, famous for its cherry blossom. I was, however, much too late for that and had to be content with the beginning of the chrysanthemum season. I met up with a Greenjacket, 'Tiger' White, whom I had known in Calcutta and we stayed together for most of the rest of our time.

Everything in Japan was extremely cheap. The yen was valued at one shilling and twopence and one could afford to stay in good hotels. We did so sometimes, but preferred the smaller non-tourist hotels with an occasional Japanese inn for a change.

We only spent two days in Tokyo and found that quite enough. We stayed at the old Imperial Hotel. It was built to withstand earthquakes and had enormously thick walls. The whole thing looked like a fortress. At that time it was the number one hotel of Tokyo.

We now moved to Lake Chouzengi. The British Ambassador and others of the Diplomatic Corps had houses by the lakeside and came up in the summer. There was an excellent hotel which, because of the cheapness of the yen, was within our reach. We had only intended to stay for two or three days, but the scenery and the walks were so lovely that we stayed a week.

Tiger White then had to leave for home. I had a little longer and decided to go round Mount Fuji. I started at the luxury Fujiyama Hotel, costing the equivalent of 10/- a day all in. And then I roughed it! I went round the foot of the mountain, then by boat over the lakes and by bus or walking in between them. I stayed each night at a Japanese inn.

Now it was time for me also to think of catching my boat for home. I had to take a small boat from Yokohama to Shanghai where I would pick up the Lloyd Triestino boat which was to take me to Bombay. It all sounded easy after the travelling that I had done. It was here, however, that the possibilities of trouble started. While I had been away the Italian campaign against

Ethiopia hotted up and I was about to take an Italian boat from Shanghai! I consulted the British Consul at Yokohama. There should be no problem until I met my Italian ship at Shanghai and the Consul advised me to consult the Consul-General's office at Shanghai for the latest situation and advice. The Shanghai office advised me to go ahead and check the situation when I reached Hong Kong. In the event I had no problem and in due course I reached Bombay.

Now it was back to work. Colonel Congreve was a charming man to serve. Sadly, during his second year in Bombay he became unwell. He had some obscure medical condition which got progressively worse. Perhaps it was a type of 'Parkinsons'. Soon he had to give up his command and return to the UK. Jock Hasted was sent out from England to take over command.

When the time came round again for my leave I decided to accept my sister Evelyn's invitation to visit her in Australia. She and her husband were toying with the idea of settling there to farm. My brother-in-law was, therefore, working on a farm close to Adelaide. In fact a farming career was quite unsuitable for him. He had had an accident in Africa and was not 100% fit.

The plan was that I should meet up with my sister at Adelaide and then that we should motor through Melbourne and Canberra to Sydney, staying with friends of hers on the way.

I set off as planned, but events soon overtook me. It is only a few days between Bombay and Colombo but that was quite sufficient for me to be completely bowled over! Somebody very special was on the good ship *Narkunda*! I had planned to go ashore at Colombo but my eyes were now focused on one person. They continued to be and a friendship developed. Every day it got stronger and stronger. For me the voyage was wonderful. The best of things seem to need a pause. Mine was Julia's need to get back to New Zealand in time for her brother's wedding. She was booked to fly across Australia and then on to New Zealand. Cables passed and it became possible for her to meet my sister Evelyn en route. Evelyn fell in love with her immediately, as I had done.

I was invited to New Zealand. There was no hesitation in my reply. I shortened my visit to Evelyn, who, having met Julia, quite understood.

Evelyn and I drove across from Adelaide to Sydney and, after a few days there, I was on a ship on the way to Julia. The voyage seemed endless, but eventually we were there and Julia was waiting on the quay. Then we were into her car and on our way to Hawkes Bay. There were ten thousand things to talk about.

It had been decided that I should stay at an hotel in Napier and that Julia would pick me up in the morning and take me to meet the family. In the morning Julia was there and we set off for Lindisfarne, a large colonial-style house on the outskirts of Hastings. Julia's mother was in the garden pruning the roses. I could not really have been very welcome. It must be a shock for one's daughter to want to marry an unknown man and go to live some 12,000 miles away from her home and family. How happy, I believe, her parents would have been if they could have been with us fifty years later when we were celebrating our Golden Wedding, after fifty years of unbelievably happy married life.

The time was approaching for me to return to India and it was decided that I should return in a year to get married. In due course my P & O boat deposited me at Bombay. It took great patience to continue the routine life as Adjutant in Bombay.

CHAPTER VIII

The Sudan and Marriage

Now we heard that we would be moving to Khartoum at the end of the year. This involved a great deal of work for the Adjutant, preparing a changeover from the India establishment to the UK one used in the Sudan. For example, we had no mechanical transport of any sort in India. We used mules, horses and horse-drawn carts. On arrival in the Sudan we would be confronted with some sixty lorries. The soldiers would have to be trained to drive and maintain them.

Fortunately all went well. The ship arrived and our accommodation and stores were checked and taken over by the incoming Battalion. An exhausted Adjutant was among the last to embark. We disembarked at Port Sudan and then went on, by rail, to Khartoum where we found good barracks awaiting us.

While I was serving as Adjutant I was, at the same time, working for the Staff College exam which would be held early in the New Year. In India the normal practice was to take one of the very comprehensive correspondence courses organized professionally from the UK, and at the same time to attend one of the short courses arranged by the various Headquarters in India. There was no question of my being able to spare the time to attend a course in India, but I decided to enrol in a UK correspondence course.

Shortly after I got back from New Zealand in 1936 I received a very large and heavy parcel containing the papers, or at least some of them, that I would be required to work through, plus a considerable bill. Weighing the parcel up in my hands, I realized that I would have no chance of getting through all that work at the same time as doing my job as Adjutant. I accordingly re-addressed the parcel and sent it back to the senders unopened. Fortunately I had made no commitment. At Khartoum I was in luck. The General there had been on the Directing Staff at Camberley and was very kind in helping candidates. Entirely due to him, I qualified well, but, as was usual in those days, did not get a competitive vacancy and took the exam again the following year.

All this time my thoughts were naturally on Julia and New Zealand and our coming marriage. Now I was about to give up the Adjutantcy and I could forget about the Staff College. I would soon be on my way to Julia.

I left Khartoum in the middle of April and set sail from Port Sudan on the long voyage to New Zealand. I was met in Australia by my sister Evelyn who saw me off on the boat which would take me across to Wellington where Julia met me. We were married on 26 May, 1937.

In June, after our honeymoon, we embarked for England on the *Remuera*, and headed for the Panama Canal and home. In mid-Atlantic a sad blow struck us both. I received a telegram to say that my mother had just died. She had been looking forward to meeting Julia and it was a great disappointment that they never had a chance to meet.

On our return to England my first task was to settle the various business matters that naturally arose. Later we settled into an Army quarter at Woking, where the Battalion was stationed, during which time our daughter Joanna was born.

CHAPTER IX

War is declared

On our return to England the Staff College was a hive of activity and within a few days war was declared. We were kept busy digging trenches and shelters. While arrangements were being made for our wartime appointments, we were sent off to our regimental depots, and I duly travelled north to Brancepeth Castle in Co. Durham.

At Brancepeth there followed a rather frustrating two weeks. I was only a lodger at the depot and was employed in preparing and running exercises. I was expecting a summons to take up a staff appointment and soon it came. I was to be a General Staff Officer at the War Office. This was good news. I was to report immediately to a branch known as Staff Duties 2. Our responsibilities were overseas organization and weapons and equipment. I was promoted to the rank of Major and became the General Staff Officer, 2nd Grade (GSO 2).

At the beginning the main part of my work was the allocation of weapons to the different theatres and units. Weapons were in very short supply and deciding on priorities was no easy job.

At the beginning of May, 1940, my work took me to GHQ in France. I had barely got off the boat at Dover, on my return, when the great German assault on France and Belgium started. When I got back to London I appealed to my General to release me from the War Office so that I could join a Field Formation. This was agreed, but it was some time before a relief for me could be found. The situation in France had become very serious and the evacuation from Dunkirk was beginning. Eventually I was appointed GSO 2 of the 2nd Division. The Division had just got back from Dunkirk and was reforming in the East Riding of Yorkshire. A German attempt at invasion was expected at any time and we were very much on our toes.

Our Divisional HQ was at Pocklington and we were responsible for a long stretch of the Yorkshire coast. The area was thought to be vulnerable and there were constant practices and alerts. Then, early in September, there came a major invasion alert with the code name 'Cromwell'. For some days all troops were stood to.

Just at that time Simon was born. Arrangements had been made that this baby should be born at the Woking Nursing Home. A telegram announcing the arrival of Simon came almost at the same time as the alert. I thought that there would be no chance of my being able to get down to see Julia; but as luck would have it, the alert was suddenly called off.

I spent two days with Julia before returning to Yorkshire. We decided that, as soon as she had recovered from the birth, she, Nanny and the two children should come to Yorkshire and that in the meantime I would look for accommodation for them.

On my return to Yorkshire I found that I had been lucky to get away. The alert had been reimposed almost immediately after I left but was now lifted. The Division was still as watchful as ever and intensive training was going on everywhere.

Our number one Officers' Mess was at Warter Priory, a very large house and splendid garden belonging to the Vesteys. After a little negotiation it was agreed that I should rent the butler's cottage in the grounds, as soon as Julia was able to travel. The accommodation was a little basic but it would do for the time being.

The time left to me in Yorkshire proved to be all too short. A telegram arrived to say that I was to report to the War Office immediately for an appointment in the Staff Duties Directorate. My General was as upset as I was and we both appealed to the War Office, but got no change. When I arrived at the War Office I was sent for by the Director of Staff Duties, General Nye. He made it quite clear to me that my job was to serve where I was most wanted. In fact he was extremely kind to me. During my time on his staff I formed a great respect for him.

Now came the problem of where Julia was to live, for at this time the Blitz was at its height. Julia had an invitation from the Carlyons who lived at Tregrehan in Cornwall for herself, Nanny and the children. The Carlyons were old friends of Julia's family in New Zealand. The stay was a great success. The Carlyons were very kind to her and she was very happy with them, staying for more than a year.

CHAPTER X

The War Office 1940-1942

Soon after I reached London a friend in my branch at the War Office told me of a friend of his who had a large house in Cadogan Square. She had just lost her husband and would probably welcome me as a paying guest. I went to see her and thus started a close friendship. She also became very fond of Julia who was able to come up from Cornwall occasionally. Our friendship with Mrs Seary-Mercer lasted until she died in the late 1970s.

My Boss at the War Office was Colonel Brownjohn. He was a very able officer and I got on well with him. I also worked closely with General Nye. Early in 1941 Colonel Brownjohn was promoted and I was summoned by General Nye and told that I would be promoted Lieutenant-Colonel and succeed to Colonel Brownjohn. I thus became GSO 1 of the branch called Staff Duties 2. My responsibilities were for overseas organization. We handled very secret matters concerning the build-up of Orders of Battle for the overseas theatres. We were also the General Staff branch deciding on the priority of space on convoys going out to the Middle East and elsewhere. There was strong competition for convoy space and the decisions were taken at a high level. The General often detailed me to take the chair on his behalf at these meetings. Because of the secrecy of our work, I had a specially selected private secretary who worked in my office and safeguarded my papers. General Nye often put me on to interesting and important jobs which he might well have preferred to handle himself.

I remember one occasion when the make-up of the Middle East Order of Battle was challenged by the Prime Minister, who would not accept the size of the Administrative 'tail' demanded by the C-in-C, Middle East. General Nye came into my room one evening and told me that I was to go to 10 Downing Street at once and explain to the Prime Minister the details of the C-in-C's request and exactly what the units were for. I was disappointed on arrival at 10 Downing Street to be told that the PM was resting and would not be able to see me. So back I went. I was in my office at 11pm that evening when the telephone rang. It was Number 10. I was to go there at once.

I had just got into Number 10 and was standing in the hall when the PM came down the stairs with the C-in-C's paper in his hand. He did not seem in a good mood and he did not like dealing with people he did not know. It was not a good beginning. He asked me whether I had seen the paper and had mastered it. It was a long and detailed one and, although I had seen it, it had been whisked off my desk and taken to Sir John Dill, the CIGS. However, I acknowledged having mastered it! The PM then took me into the Cabinet Room and sat me down beside him. He questioned me searchingly on everything in the paper, 'Why this?', 'Why that?' and a host of detailed questions. He had seemed rather hostile at the start, but began to thaw when he discovered that I could answer his questions. I was asked whether I would like a whisky and soda, I said yes please, and he then became very agreeable. After about an hour he told me to take the paper away and write in the margin everything I had told him and then send it back. The PM then started walking up and down behind the table, talking about the war and criticizing a recent withdrawal that had taken place in the Middle East. I unwisely drew attention to the lack of administrative backing. The PM's reply was, 'Nonsense, bad Generalship,' meaning General Wavell. I then had a most interesting half-hour with him. I had got on well with the PM, and Brigadier Joe Hollis from the Cabinet Secretariat, who was present, told General Nye that the meeting had been a success. As a result I was rung up again by the Cabinet Secretariat asking me to come over for another meeting, but I had to say that the subject was not mine.

We had now reached a period of the Blitz in London when the Germans put on two or three large-scale raids each month. They were most unpleasant. Cadogan Square seemed often to be in the target area. There were many fires in the Square and the fire and other services could only cope with them in turn. One could see fire bombs on the balconies in the square and these had to be pushed into the street before they took hold. One night a fire bomb dropped in the gutter of a house nearby, but the window was protected by iron bars and none of us was thin enough to get through the bars. Eventually a little girl was found who could squeeze through and push the bomb into the street with a spade.

The most troublesome evening I had was the night before the great fire in the City. I had been given a rare weekend leave. Julia was in Cornwall and I was to go down by train to see her. Then a full-scale raid started. The Underground ceased to run. There were no buses and no taxis. I set off to walk from Cadogan Square to Paddington carrying my bag. It was a most unpleasant journey. When I reached Paddington there were fires all round the station and considerable doubt as to whether any trains were going to run. I was lucky. Eventually one train set off for Cornwall and I was on it!

I had a splendid weekend with Julia and the children. It was all too short and I returned to London on the Monday. The City fire was now pretty well under control, but it had done an immense amount of damage.

The Middle East situation throughout the summer was bad and events in Greece and Crete had gone seriously wrong. That summer was in every way an anxious time. The Germans had invaded Russia and it seemed that this at least might turn to their disadvantage.

Then, at the beginning of December, 1941, the Japanese attacked Pearl Harbor. The immediate results were disastrous to the Americans but it brought America into the war which, in the end, proved decisive.

It was decided that there should be a meeting between the PM and the President in Washington before Christmas, at which the Chiefs of Staff of the two countries would be present, to discuss the future conduct of the war. There was great activity in Whitehall preparing briefs in readiness. The PM and the rest of the British delegation then set off in the battleship *Duke of York*.

After the PM's party had been in Washington for a few days it appeared that the discussions might become more detailed than at first thought and a telegram was sent to London instructing that Geoff Bourne of the Plans Directorate and myself from the Staff of General Nye should be sent out at once along with a representative of the Ministry of Transport and one from the Air Ministry. I rushed down to Camberley to say goodbye to Julia and collect a few clothes. Then the four of us set off for Washington.

A special train was waiting for us at Euston. We travelled to

Prestwick in great luxury. In addition to a sleeper we had a restaurant car and ordinary day carriages. We were seen off by the Station Master in his top hat! On arrival at Prestwick we were taken to the RAF Station HQ and fitted out with RAF flying suits. We were to make the Atlantic crossing in a Liberator bomber and we were told the drill we should follow in the aircraft and particularly for the use of oxygen masks. We would be flying at more than 18,000 feet and would need oxygen throughout. If we wanted to move about the aircraft for any purpose, we would need to plug in our oxygen masks to one of the points on our route.

The aircraft was pretty uncomfortable. There were no seats. We would sit on the floor and do our best to sleep. As soon as we had been briefed by the RAF we embarked and took off.

After flying for about three hours a member of the crew came back with a message from the Captain. He said that one of the engines was not performing well and he regretted that he would have to return to base. In due course we touched down at Prestwick and returned to the RAF Mess. We were anxious, during this delay, that it would be decided that we were not needed after all! Fortunately all went well and, after a delay of several hours, we were off. This time there was no problem. Our first stop was in Newfoundland where we were given an enormous breakfast. None of us had seen so much food since the beginning of the war. Then we were off again for Washington. It was Christmas. We were accommodated at the Wardman Park Hotel with the rest of the Delegation. I shared a very comfortable suite with Geoff Bourne.

Soon after we arrived I was told that Mrs Beaumont-Nesbitt, wife of the Military Attache, had kindly offered to do some shopping and I was advised to ask for nylon stockings which were the latest thing. I bought two dozen pairs which were very popular when I got home. Geoff had been asked by his wife for some cami-knickers. When we had a chance, we searched Washington for these garments, but failed utterly! It appeared that American ladies did not wear such things. I had much the same trouble trying to buy biscuits. What we call biscuits are either crackers or cookies!

By January the war situation had become very black. Our two remaining battleships in Malayan waters were sunk by Japanese naval aircraft and Singapore fell. These losses greatly affected the discussion on future plans. A North Africa campaign was under consideration, but doubt was inevitably cast on what we were capable of doing. Then the time came for the whole party to return to the UK.

Most of us had spent a great deal of money on things to take home. I had also spent a lot on telephone calls to my sister Evelyn in California. When the day came to leave, we were told that we were not to tell the hotel that we were off, nor, for security reasons, were we to settle our hotel bills. This was splendid news for me. I felt sure, however, that our hotel bills would catch up before long. They never did. We learnt that all our expenses, including the dollars we had been given on our arrival, were to be written off as 'lend lease'.

With the PM's party we joined a special train for Norfolk, Virginia, and there we were met by several flying boats which took us all to Bermuda. The PM had enjoyed his flight and decided to continue in the same flying boat to the UK. He took with him the Chiefs of Staff. For security reasons the rest of us were to wait at Bermuda until the PM's arrival in England. Lord Knollys, who was Governor of Bermuda at the time, had come to Washington to see the Prime Minister while he was there. I met him on the train on the way to Norfolk. His wife Margaret was a connection of mine by marriage and they invited me to stay at Government House while we were waiting confirmation of the PM's arrival in England.

Eventually we embarked on the *Duke of York* and set sail for England with a very impressive escort of warships. Because so many had gone with the PM by flying boat, we were very comfortably accommodated on the *Duke of York*. I had Lord Beaverbrook's cabin with a private bathroom.

Soon after I got back from Washington I spoke to General Nye about the possibility of regimental duty with a view to obtaining command of a Battalion of my Regiment. The General was sympathetic and knew that this was what I ought to do. So far my war service had been mostly at the War Office. He promised to talk to the Military Secretary and ask what was coming up in my Regiment.

Before long I found myself appointed to command the 11th

Battalion of the Durham Light Infantry. This was a great thrill. Command of one's Regiment is the ambition of every soldier. I was extremely grateful to General Nye and I knew how much trouble he had taken over my appointment. When I went to say goodbye he told me that the Military Secretary had undertaken that I should not be appointed again to the Staff until the war was over. Sure enough I remained with the soldiers until I was in Semarang in February, 1946, when I was appointed Director of Plans. General Nye wrote to me about this and reminded me of his promise. He had fulfilled it most kindly.

I remained in command of the 11th Battalion for just over a year and enjoyed it enormously. During that time we were stationed in many different places all over the UK. We were part of the 70th Brigade of the 49th Division. I took over the Battalion in Herefordshire but soon moved to Wales. Then we were in Scotland for a short time and then in Llanelli.

A short time after I joined the Battalion, I needed a Second-in-Command. There were several regular officers within the Battalion and the Brigade Commander thought that one of these ought to be selected. There was, however, one outstanding young Territorial officer. He had joined the Battalion from journalism as a 2nd Lieutenant just before the war. He had been with the Battalion in France before Dunkirk, and then in Iceland with them. He was obviously a very high-grade young man. I gave myself a month before taking the matter up with the Brigadier. By that time I was quite sure that we had an exceptional officer. His appointment would involve passing over regular officers who were reasonably qualified. The Brigadier was rather doubtful but he agreed and the appointment was confirmed. Denis Hamilton was the man. He proved his worth throughout the war, being selected, in due course, to command the Battalion and later, when there was a reorganisation in the Division, to command a Battalion of the Duke of Wellington's Regiment. After the war, returning to journalism, he became Personal Assistant to Lord Kelmsley and later editor of the *Sunday Times* and Chairman of Times Newspapers, Chairman of Reuters and a number of other important City organisations. He became a close friend of mine.

During our training we all realized that we were destined for the 'Second Front', which could not be long delayed. This naturally put spice into our training and, indeed, everything we did. There were many long and realistic exercises and we got ourselves extremely fit.

CHAPTER XI

The 5th Parachute Brigade

At Llanelli one morning early in May, 1943, I went into my office and found waiting for me a letter from the Military Secretary at the War Office telling me that I had been selected to command a Parachute Brigade and asking whether I was prepared to parachute. It was a complete surprise. Parachuting had never entered my mind.

It happened that Julia had come to Llanelli to be with me for a few days. I rushed off to tell her the news. She did not have quite the same enthusiasm as me, but she did not try to dissuade me. I then went to see my Brigadier. He had not heard from the War Office and advised me to think it over. He said that he knew that I was about to become a Brigadier but he had no idea of the Parachute Brigade.

Of course it needed no thought by me. The Airborne Forces were a *corps d'élite*. Every parachutist was a volunteer. The tests for selection were strict. When the airborne soldier won his red beret and wings he was a proud man. My reply to the Military Secretary went back within the hour. In no time joining instructions reached me. I was to form the 5th Parachute Brigade at Bulford, which would be part of the 6th Airborne Division which was being raised at the same time.

In due course I stepped out of a train at Andover, properly dressed as a Brigadier, and was met by Ted Lough, my Administrative Staff Officer, who was to become a firm friend for life. John Barker, who was to be my Brigade Major, was also at the station. We set off for Bulford with a Parachute Brigade pennant fluttering on the bonnet of the car.

Divisional HQ, which had been formed a month or so before, was in the midst of an exercise without troops, designed, if I remember, to fit the different branches of the staff into their operational roles. General Gale sent a message through my Brigade

Major that he would like me to join him at the exercise and the next day I set out for General Gale's exercise. I spent a day and a night with them.

It was then decided that within the next ten days or so I should go to Hardwick Hall and Ringway to do my parachute training. Hardwick was where the fitness training took place before going on to Ringway, where the parachute course was held. Both were pretty tough. I spent the next ten days visiting my three Battalions and the other Brigade units. It was extremely difficult for any officer or man to get into a parachute unit. An officer would have an extensive interview with the Brigadier, and a soldier would have other equivalent tests. At any time an officer or man could be returned to regimental duty if not up to the mark.

My 7th (Light Infantry) Parachute Battalion was an experienced parachute battalion transferred into my Brigade. The other two were territorial battalions in which the men who wished to volunteer for parachuting and came up to the standard remained on. The rest of the men were made up from volunteers from the Army as a whole.

I was pretty fit when I went to Hardwick but soon realized that the standard of fitness required in the Parachute Regiment was well above anything I had experienced. This unfortunately tested my damaged knee more than it would stand. I had had to be careful at my preliminary medical examination, before joining the Brigade, that the MO did not discover this weakness, but when it blew up to a very large size at Hardwick, there was no concealing it. However, the authorities were kind and I was excused exercises that tested it too much. At the end I was given a very good report for the course. I did not see this report until about a year ago when it was produced from the archives for my amusement and, indeed, my surprise.

The parachute course at Ringway was easier for me than Hardwick had been. Seven jumps were needed to qualify as a parachutist. The first two were balloon jumps. At the end there was a final night jump. Curiously, many disliked the balloon jumps. People found them rather cold-blooded. They missed the rush of air and the general excitement inside the aircraft. The balloon jumps were, however, much safer. The ground on which one landed had been carefully selected and there were no trees to fall into!

All the aircraft jumps were done from a Whitley bomber. A hole had been cut in the floor of the fuselage. The hole was not over-large in circumference and, to make a safe exit, it was necessary to sit rigid on the edge of the hole before launching oneself into it. Anyone who looked down or was in any way bent risked hitting his face on the opposite side. He would end up with a bloody mark on his chin or nose, known as ringing the bell. There is no doubt that the first to jump had an advantage; he had plenty of time to steady himself while waiting for the 'Red' warning light to come on and then the 'Green' to 'Go', that is 'jump'. The technique was to have one's hands at the back of the hole and push off, keeping the body rigid until the parachute opened.

The jumping drill was a bit more complicated than I have perhaps described. A well-trained parachutist should be able to control the direction of his flight by pulling on the lift webs of his parachute and land into the wind with a roll. He should descend with his feet and knees together so as to help with this roll. During his descent he should be looking out for landmarks, so that on landing he knows where he is. I regret to say that I was seldom able to do any of these things.

While I was at Ringway Brigadier Hugh Kindersley came to do a parachute jump. There was no need for him to do one, as his was a Glider Brigade, but he wanted the experience. It was decided that he should do a jump into water. This would give him all the experience in the aircraft but reduce the chance of injury. I was asked whether I would like to jump with him and accepted. We were to do our jump into a lake at Tatton Park near Ringway. Before getting into the aircraft we were carefully briefed, put on suitable clothes, then our Mae Wests and parachutes. When all this had been checked, we emplaned and took off. We flew the short distance to the lake, then took up 'Action Stations'. There was a bellow of 'Go!' from the instructor and one by one we were out. The first parachute jump is always exciting, but there were no problems, a gentle descent into the water. The boats came to each of us in turn. Then a hot cup of tea from a thermos, into the bus and back to our quarters and a bath. All so simple one could hardly believe it.

Hugh Kindersley, Commander of the Airlanding Brigade, was older than the other two of us Brigade Commanders. He had fought in the First War and was liked and respected throughout the Division. Sadly he and Lord Lovat, Commander of the 1st Commando Brigade, were both badly wounded at the Battle for Breville on the night of 12 June, 1944, only six days after our land ing in Normandy. They came under shellfire while watching the attack develop and their wounds necessitated their immediate evacuation. It proved to be the end of their war. Hugh inherited the title of Lord Kindersley and went on to become Chairman of Lazards, the Merchant Bankers, also Chairman of Rolls Royce and a number of other important City Institutions. Kindersley's departure was a sad loss to the 6th Airborne Division.

Following the water jump, I completed the seven jumps required without incident. Then there was a period of two weeks' leave. This was given to all who completed the Ringway course. It was a good thing as it gave everyone a chance to unwind after what was a hard and intensive course. I was particularly glad of the leave as it helped my knee to recover from the battering it had had at Hardwick and Ringway.

Now all my interest and activity were directed once more towards the training of my Battalions and the other units in my Brigade. There was a real purpose in all we did and we realized that time was short. The visits we received made this apparent. First, King George VI and the Queen and the two Princesses came round the whole Division and saw some of the work being done. Then we had a visit from Monty. He inspected us; then all the troops were told to crowd round his jeep while he addressed us.

We specialized in night work, going out in small parties over long distances across country. On one occasion I arranged with Downside School to end up there after night advances lasting about seven days. I took a party of ten from my Brigade HQ and we set off from Bulford. We moved only at night and slept as well as we could in barns by day.

About this time the 101st U.S. Airborne Division came to the Newbury area. We were twinned with them and got to know them well. Colonel Robert Sink was my opposite number and when I went to call on him, he suggested that I should do a jump with his Regiment. Their jumping technique was slightly different to ours and during my descent the countryside nearby must have been well alerted by the bellows from the instructor. Not long after, I believe that the Americans adopted our technique of 'feet and knees together'.

On my return to Bulford, I looked in on a balloon jump by the 13th Battalion. Just as I reached them, one of the very rare parachuting accidents occurred, a fault known as a 'Roman Candle'. The poor man was killed. A parachute failure can be

5 Field-Marshal Montgomery visits the 6th Armoured Division in the
Ardennes during the Battle of the Bulge (see p.82). The author on Montgomery's left.

6 The liberation of Pont L'Evêque, 24 August, 1944. "The fierceness of the
fighting can be judged by the sad destruction of houses throughout the
town" (p.80).

7 "Without a doubt the great feature of my time at the Staff College was
the visit of the Queen, accompanied by Prince Philip, on 23 April, 1958"
(p.127). With Prince Philip is Brigadier David Peel-Yates.

8 "An interesting guest was the German General Hans Spiedel, C-in-C
Allied Land Forces in Central Europe" (p.129). On the left is Major-
General Jack Churcher.

unsettling to others present. It was the custom for the Senior Officer present to go up immediately and do a jump. I had done a jump with my Brigade H.Q. in the early morning, then came my jump with the Americans, so this was my third that day.

CHAPTER XII

Training with 6th Airborne Division

At the end of February, 1944, General Browning briefed General Gale on the plans for the long-awaited Second Front. Codenamed 'Overlord', it was a seaborne assault against the Normandy Coast, extending from the Caen Canal westwards to the Cherbourg Peninsula. The American Army would be on the right and the British on the left.

The 6th Airborne Division would have the important role of securing the Allied left flank. We would be under command of the British 1st Corps. General Gale could now set about developing his plan.

The first priority task of the Division was to seize the bridges over the Caen Canal and the River Orne at Benouville and Ranville and to establish a bridgehead, in depth, to cover these crossings. The bridgehead must be secured and held at any cost. These bridges were the only crossing places between Caen and the sea. Their loss would isolate the 6th Airborne Division from the seaborne landings west of the canal and endanger the whole of the Allied left flank. The bridgehead was also required for the development of future operations. West of the canal the bridgehead must be held until relieved by the 3rd British Division, landing on the beaches. Relief for the bridgehead east of the Orne would come from the 6th Airlanding Brigade whose gliders would land at 9 p.m. on the evening of D-Day.

The Orne crossing places were equally important to the Germans who would want access for their reserves to counter-attack the flank of the Allied landings. They were certain to reply vigorously to our assault.

My 5th Parachute Brigade was given the task of seizing the bridges and securing the bridgehead in depth. This was a role of great importance. The priority task for Brigadier James Hill's 3rd Parachute Brigade was to silence the guns of a strongly defended

Coast Defence Battery to the north - the Merville Battery. This Battery could engage our troops landing on the beaches near Ouistreham. The Battery was required to be neutralized half an hour before first light. Hill's Brigade was also to destroy the bridges over the River Dives, in order to slow up the movement of German Reserves towards the area of the seaborne landings. Finally, Hill was to occupy the ridge running northwards from Troarn towards Sallenelles which overlooked the ground north of Ranville and the beaches close to Ouistreham.

Hugh Kindersley's Glider Brigade would fly in a second lift on 6 June, landing at 9 p.m. He was then to extend the depth of the 5 Para Brigade bridgehead to the south and south-east of Le Bas de Ranville and Herouvillette.

All this planning for the 6th Airborne was highly secret. Nationwide, there was a deception plan designed to mislead the Germans on the location of the coming assault. The purpose was to attract the attention of the Germans towards the Pas de Calais area where land-based aircraft could operate over the invasion area. Skeleton Corps, with Divisional and Unit HQ were established in the south-east of England; their equipment consisted only of wireless sets and a carefully prepared programme of messages. Great care was taken during our own exercises that nothing was given away.

General Gale, in giving me his orders, specified that, in seizing the bridges, reliance should be placed on speed and surprise and that the assault should take the form of a *coup de main*. The bridges and their defences must be rushed before the bridges could be destroyed.

The General, in studying my 5th Para Brigade problem, had concluded that only a glider-borne force could be landed sufficiently concentrated and close enough to the bridges to enable them to be rushed before the Germans could destroy them. The General accordingly placed under my command a glider-borne Company of the Oxford and Buckinghamshire Light Infantry. In due course, Major John Howard was appointed to command this Company. As time went by two extra platoons and a number of Engineers were added.

Possible landing grounds close to the bridges were very restricted in size and only three gliders could land at each bridge. It was felt, however, that provided the bulk of Howard's six platoons were landed accurately, they could hold out until relief came from a parachute battalion landing in the area north of Ranville. It would not be possible, however, to land glider-borne troops in this area as it had been obstructed by the Germans with anti-air-landing poles, which were effective against gliders but not para-troops. Some clearing would be necessary before it could be used for gliders.

I selected Lieutenant-Colonel Pine-Coffin's 7th Para Battalion to be responsible for relieving Howard's force at the bridges. Lieutenant-Colonel Johnston's 12th Para Battalion would be responsible for securing the bridgehead south and south-east of the Orne River bridge. Lieutenant-Colonel Luard's 13th Battalion was to secure the village of Ranville and also clear as much as was necessary of the poles on the landing ground, in readiness for the glider force due to land at 3.30am. This glider force would include General Gale's Tactical HQ and an urgently needed Anti-tank Gun Battery.

The speed with which the 7th Battalion could reach the bridges would depend on the accuracy with which they were dropped. The river bridge was some 1200 yards from the centre of the drop-ping zone (D.Z.) and the canal bridge 400 yards further. The accuracy of the whole Brigade drop would depend on a Path-finder group which was to land at the same time as the *coup de main* force, 20 minutes after midnight. Their task would be to put out Eureka Beacons on which the parachute aircraft would home. The Brigade group was to drop at 0050 hrs.

The simultaneous landing of the *coup de main* force and the Path-finders was an important feature of the plan. Both these groups needed surprise. This was obviously necessary for the *coup de main* and it was equally important for the Pathfinders, whose flight plan was directly over the Atlantic Wall. They would be flying at a low altitude to come in under the radar screen.

The Brigade planning went ahead on these lines. The success of the plan would depend on the accurate and safe landing of the gliders and on surprise and speed in the assault. It would also depend on the speedy relief of the *coup de main* force by the 7th Para Battalion and the development by them of an extended and secure bridgehead on the west bank. It was essential, but beyond our control, that the alertness of the German bridge sentries and garrison should be no greater than usual!

There was a considerable element of risk in the *coup de main* operation and a contingency plan was necessary in case it miscarried. The contingency plan included an assault crossing of the two waterways by the 7th Para Battalion. Detailed orders were issued to the Battalion for this operation. They carried thirty inflatable dinghies and twelve recce boats in large kit bags attached to the legs of the paratroopers and released on a cord before landing.

I decided to drop with a small command post at the same time as the Pathfinders, so that, if the *coup de main* did miscarry, I could control the contingency plan and adjust the deployment of the Brigade.

On 2 May I issued written orders to Howard for the *coup de main* operation and briefed him in detail. I then gave him a pass permitting entry to Brigmaston House where the divisional planning was done and access to all the secret Intelligence material.

During the study and planning period, security was of top importance. The 6th Airborne Division planning was done in a specially protected small house, known as Brigmaston Farm House, close to the Divisional HQ. Each brigade was allotted a room in the house. Here Intelligence summaries, maps and air photographs were kept under conditions of maximum security. An accurate scale model of the whole of the divisional area was maintained, and also detailed large-scale models of the bridges over the river and the canal, their surroundings and defences. The Intelligence material was constantly kept up to date. The number of individuals given passes to admit them to Brigmaston was kept to a minimum. Each individual was briefed at the last possible moment, consistent with his own planning and training commitments. It was here that Howard carried out all his planning. He had access to the Intelligence information available and he could ask for any information he wished.

Intensive training continued for all units of the Brigade Group. During May I went to Exeter to watch an exercise Howard had arranged for his Company. There were two bridges there over branches of the River Exe which, known only to Howard, had similarities to those in Normandy. This similarity, however, was carefully concealed from the other officers and men of the Company.

Meanwhile the specially selected glider pilots were training equally intensively. Night after night they followed the course of the operational flight plan they would use. They landed in the darkness, on tiny patches, to simulate their D-Day tasks.

On 26 May, 1944, our younger son Brian was born. He was a

fine healthy boy and by the time I left for Normandy, Julia and the baby were making excellent progress.

Our preparations and planning were now complete. As far as we could judge nothing had been left to chance. Towards the end of May the whole Brigade moved to specially sealed transit camps close to the airfields from which we would fly. Most of us were at Harwell, but Howard and his men were at Tarrant Rushton, where his tug aircraft and gliders were assembled. Officers and men were, for security reasons, not allowed to leave the camp. All the Intelligence material and briefing equipment had been assembled there. All ranks in turn were told their exact tasks on D-Day. They were able to go over, time and again, what they had to do. They examined the models and studied the maps and air photographs.

From Harwell I paid a last visit to Howard and his D Company and found them in great heart. They had been visited by Monty and assured him that they would not fail. Now we only waited the word to go.

We were delayed for a day by the weather. The next day, 5 June, the weather seemed worse. We well knew the implications of a further delay on security and on the troops who were already embarked and were tossing about in their transports. However, the word came through that the operation was 'on' that night. The relief was enormous.

Those who follow this story through the Normandy Campaign and beyond will realize that although it is told as a personal account, the achievements of the 6th Airborne Division were the achievements of the Division as a whole. Indeed they were the achievements of every single unit and of every soldier making up the 6th Airborne Division team of which we were all very proud.

CHAPTER XIII

D-Day

I think that the story of our operations is best told by an account of the doings of each unit in turn. Let us start with my Command Post and the Pathfinder Force. At 9.30pm on 5 June, the evening before D-Day, lorries drew up at our transit camp, a separate lorry for each aircraft 'stick' as we called it, to take us to the airfield from which we would fly — in our case Brize Norton.

A welcoming cup of tea and then we were alongside our aircraft. It was an Albemarle. None of my stick had ever been in one before. It was a small aircraft holding only ten paratroopers. The exit was through double doors in the floor, aft of the aircraft. These doors opened inwards and it was the task of the No. 1 — the first to jump — to lean forward over the doors and, the word having been passed back from the Captain of the aircraft, to open them. It sounded simple enough, but it was not as easy as it sounded. I was the Number 1!

We all piled in and sat on the floor facing the tail. A future problem soon became obvious. Most of the men in the 'stick' were carrying just a bit more than their normal gear, perhaps extra ammunition, extra grenades, weapons or even food. There were ten unusually fat men under their jumping jackets! We would need to be well squashed up together, to be clear of the doors in the floor, so that when the time came I could open them.

Then we settled down. It was 11pm and we were off. The visibility was moderate but the hoped-for moon was often covered and the wind stronger than we would have liked. But this was a problem, at that stage, for the pilots. We were unconscious of anything outside our closed and very uncomfortable box.

Then in due course the word was passed back, 'Open the doors'. My personal struggle then began — pushing, cursing, shoving to get enough room for me to be off the doors and able to open them, and time was slipping away as we approached the

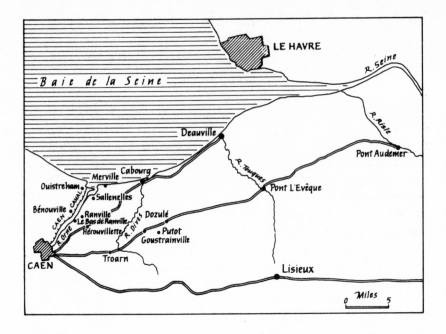

coast of France. Then success; I was leaning over the open doors. Down below me the sea looked choppy and uninviting.

Now we were speeding over the coast defences, at about 400 feet and not a shot was fired at us. Surprise was complete. The red light came on – 'prepare to jump' – then the green, 'jump' and I was out in the night air and, almost immediately, in fact some 20 seconds, a big bump. I had arrived safely on the soil of France.

It was all much too quick. I had done none of the things I ought to have done such as identifying Ranville church, or pulling on my lift webs to get a good landing, but I was down and I had not landed on top of one of Rommel's asparagus – anti-airlanding poles – set to catch us.

I had no idea where I was. It was too dark to see the church or any of the landmarks on which we had been briefed, but I could see the exhaust of the aircraft disappearing and I knew that it would be going over Ranville. I knew my direction therefore. All was black and still, not a shot had been fired.

After getting rid of my parachute, I moved in the direction of flight of my aircraft, and sure enough I came across one of my men and he and I set off in the same direction. Then almost at once, to my right, the silence and the darkness was transformed: All the sights and sounds of battle — explosions, firing, signal lights and so on.

Now I knew exactly where I was and where I must go, as fast as possible. I would have liked to have found my wireless operator and set, but it was more important to get to the bridges at once. The RV for all my stick was the river bridge and my wireless operator should meet me there later. Sadly, he didn't. He was killed on the dropping zone.

My stick had been well dropped. Wing Commander McMonnies, the Squadron Commander, had been my pilot and had done a splendid job. I now had some 1200 yards to go across country — typical agricultural land, much of it standing crops, but several roads to cross and it was very dark. We saw no one. Then, as we approached the river bridge, we had to use extra caution. Sporadic shooting and explosions were continuing and I didn't know whether the bridges were in enemy hands or ours. Soldiers can be rather trigger-happy about men approaching their posts at night. Almost at once, however, I identified our own men. The password was exchanged. I was soon with Lieutenant (now Colonel) Tod Sweeney who recorded the time as 0052 hrs, just about half an hour after my time of landing as recorded by the pilot. As I entered the bridge defended area I heard the roar of aircraft behind me — a comforting sound in the night sky. It was the main body of my Brigade beginning to come into the DZ I had just left. This drop was timed for 0050 hrs.

I spent a little time with the captors of the river bridge. They were naturally very thrilled with their achievement and were busy organizing their defences. They told me that John Howard's assault on the canal bridge had gone equally well and that he was established on both sides of the canal. My companion and I then set off to cover the 400 yards between the two bridges.

In the excitement of meeting up at the river bridge, John Howard's Platoon Commander had not told him of my arrival, nor that I was on my way to see him. He was surprised, and a little put out, as I walked unexpectedly into his position. But he was so thrilled with his success, and with my very warm congratulations, that his Platoon Commander was quickly forgiven.

Howard told me his glider pilots had been magnificent. His

own glider had been landed exactly as he planned, with its nose into the wire defences of the bridge. As was inevitable, it was a crash landing but he and his men soon recovered. Every man knew his exact job. In no time they were out of the glider and streaming off to their assault tasks. Meanwhile, the next and then the next glider — all had found their tiny landing patch with the greatest accuracy.

The young officer who was leading the assault across the bridge at the head of his men was mortally wounded, but his men went on. Grenades had been thrown into the German pillbox and other defences, and the sten guns and other weapons of Howard's men responded to any movement. Within 10 minutes the bridge was firmly in our hands. The platoon's pre-planned positions were taken up and slit trenches were being prepared against the German patrol and counterattacks which would follow soon.

When I reached Howard, stronger efforts were already being made by the Germans to regain the bridges. One of these included a tank. The tank was most effectively dealt with by a PIAT (an infantry anti-tank weapon firing a powerful bomb). It was a short-range weapon and complicated to reload. It was, therefore, essentially a one-shot weapon in action, requiring a cool head and steady hand, plus a great deal of courage in facing a tank at close range. Howard's Sergeant Thornton had all of these qualities. He held his fire until certain of a hit and then got the tank plumb in the middle. The PIAT projectile penetrated the tank and then began to set off ammunition inside it. As it continued to turn, it provided something of a firework display.

The burning tank appears to have led the Germans to think that the bridge was more strongly held than it was. It also made Colonel Pine-Coffin, who was to relieve Howard with his 7th L.I. Parachute Battalion, very conscious of the urgency of the situation.

The drop of the main body of the brigade, which I had heard coming in at 0050, was not as accurate as hoped. For a variety of reasons, in particular the poor weather and visibility, a few of the guiding beacons had been put out too far to the east. This, with the high wind, resulted in some of the men dropping in the more difficult country off the dropping zone and further from their RV. The heavy and clumsy kitbags containing the rubber boats also complicated the exit from the aircraft and caused some long sticks. They were then an extra load in moving to the RV.

By the time the main body came in, the German posts in the DZ area were fully alerted. The reader can imagine the scene of more than 2,000 men, dropped in darkness, in a single massed drop. The men of the three battalions and of other units of the Brigade Group being mixed up and scattered on and off the DZ, the whole being a scene of some confusion as the men of the different units sorted themselves out, and in the very poor visibility searched for their RVs. The heavy weapons and equipment of the battalions had been parachuted in containers from the bomb bays of the aircraft at the same time as the men. Many containers had fallen in the standing corn. In the darkness, and with very little moonlight to help, not much of this heavy equipment was found until daylight. The absence of mortars, medium machine guns and particularly wireless sets was to prove a serious loss to the battalions when they came to repel the German attacks in the morning.

In fact all the units had done extremely well on the DZ, but it must have been after 2am that Pine-Coffin had assembled sufficient of his men to move to the bridges. Their arrival there was urgent. He could wait no longer, so, leaving his 2 I/C to bring on the rest of the Battalion, he set off at the double.

The men on the bridges had heard the aircraft of the main body fly in. Now, in their thinly-held positions and with the expectation of an attack in strength by the Germans, the delay seemed to them even longer than it was.

Pine-Coffin with his weak companies reached the canal bridge shortly after 2.30am. His War Diary records it as earlier and Howard's as later. The conditions and the darkness made it difficult to consult watches.

While Pine-Coffin's men were moving over the bridge to their pre-planned positions to extend the bridgehead to cover Le Port and Benouville, Howard briefed him on his own dispositions and the enemy activity. Pine-Coffin then took over command of the bridgehead, including Howard's Company.

With Pine-Coffin's men in position on the west bank, I felt confident that, for the time being, the bridgehead would be secure from the west. I, therefore, left the canal bridge and made for Ranville to see how the 13th Battalion had fared.

I soon met up with Peter Luard, the Battalion Commander. He was in splendid heart. He had had little difficulty in over-running the village and he was now in the course of 'mopping up' some of the houses which had been occupied by the Germans. He had established his defences on the outskirts of the village. Ranville had been captured at about 2.30am. It is, therefore, claimed to be the first village to be liberated in France.

Luard's Battalion and the Brigade engineers, 591 Para Field Squadron, were preparing runways through the poles of Rommel's asparagus to receive the gliders of General Gale's Tactical HQ, due to begin landing at 0320 hrs. This glider group would also include an urgently needed 6-pounder battery of anti-tank guns for my Brigade. 13 Para would be responsible for the protection of the landing zone for the glider landing.

After going round some of the 13 Para positions, I was entirely satisfied and was able to move on to Johnston's 12 Para. They were to hold the southern sector of the bridgehead, east of the River Orne, including Le Bas de Ranville and were hard at work preparing their defensive positions. We knew they had a tough time ahead. They would bear the brunt of any attack from 21 Panzer Division which had been moved close to Caen just before D-Day. 12 Para must, therefore, expect strong armoured and infantry attacks as soon as it was light enough for the Germans to assess the situation. The Battalion had only a short time to prepare themselves and they were certainly making the most of it.

While I was approaching the 12th Battalion General Gale's glider group began to land. After satisfying myself that all was well with the 12th, I walked back to the DZ in the hope of meeting General Gale and briefing him on the situation of my brigade. By now it was just beginning to show the first traces of light and I had not been long on the DZ before I saw the distinctive figure of the General. He was wearing jodhpur riding breeches and had about six men with him. I was able to tell him that the operations of the 5th Parachute Brigade had been entirely successful. The bridges were in our hands, intact, and all my battalions were in their pre-planned positions. Casualties so far had been light.

I now made for my HQ being set up in the grounds of the Château de Ranville. I knew that Guy Radmore, my excellent signals officer, would have established communications with the battalions and would be in touch with Divisional HQ when that was set up. My Brigade Major also had everything well under control and I was given a full picture of the work going ahead to strengthen the defences all round the Brigade area.

Let us now return to the Benouville bridgehead to see how

Pine-Coffin with his 7th Battalion and Howard's Company were getting on. It will be remembered that we left Pine-Coffin shortly before 3am extending his bridgehead in greater depth. When he judged that his men were in the positions planned, he withdrew Howard's Company, placing them in reserve between the two bridges with responsibility for the river bridge and the ground between the bridges, and with a counter-attack role.

It was not long after Pine-Coffin's Battalion was in position that the German pressure increased. Attacks in Company strength supported by tanks, self-propelled guns and armoured cars were mounted at intervals against two of Pine-Coffin's companies. By first light his left-hand company was under heavy pressure. There was no wireless contact between them and Battalion HQ and the company appeared to be surrounded.

The position as reported by the Battalion Intelligence Officer, Bertie Mills, who had worked his way through to them, was that the Medical Aid Post in the company area was overrun. The Medical Officer was missing and the Padre had been killed.

Soon after daylight the right-hand company was also heavily attacked in their position on the wooded escarpment to the west. The company was also much troubled by snipers in Le Port itself: later twelve dead Germans were found in the church tower there.

This right-hand company were finding it difficult to maintain their hold on the escarpment and were only able to dominate the southern half of Le Port. There was no communication with the battle outposts. Although they had authority to retire if need be, none did. Pine-Coffin's plan was to hold the enemy on the line of the road running north-south from Le Port to Benouville.

During the course of the day's fighting the enemy launched eight separate attacks, mostly supported by tanks or self-propelled guns, in addition to nagging constantly with small parties and occasionally armoured cars. A problem for the CO was the flank north of his HQ, extending to the bank of the canal and round Le Port, covered only by Battalion HQ personnel and a small reserve he had established.

At about 9.30am I went with General Gale on a visit to 7th Battalion HQ. On the way to Pine-Coffin, General Gale had the opportunity of congratulating Howard on the success of his *coup de main* operation. Hugh Kindersley was with us. He was waiting for the arrival of his Glider Brigade due at 9pm that night. The General found Pine-Coffin and his men in fine form, in spite of the hammering they were getting. He was left in no doubt that Pine-Coffin would hold his position.

Towards 12 noon the sound of bagpipes could be heard in the distance. This would be the first contact with the seaborne landings. It was Lord Lovat's Commando Brigade who were to pass through Pine-Coffin's Battalion and then, crossing the bridges, move to their own task on the left of the 3rd Parachute Brigade. The pipes were an exceedingly welcome sound to all of us who were with Pine-Coffin, who could not give the call on the bugle to indicate that the route to the bridges was clear. It was indeed very far from clear. However, the leading Commando had succeeded in penetrating the German forces surrounding Le Port, and were able to assist, at least temporarily, in clearing Le Port before moving on to the canal and river bridges.

General Gale, who had left Pine-Coffin some time before the arrival of the Commandos, had returned to his HQ. There he had found that my 12th Para Battalion were under very heavy pressure from armour and infantry of the 21st Panzer Division. At several places the Battalion had been forced to pull back and it seemed to the General that the river bridge was being threatened. He accordingly held back one Commando as a reserve near the bridge and at the same time sent a signal to me at Pine-Coffin's HQ telling me of the situation. I went at once to the 12th and found that they were putting up a stout resistance and they soon regained the ground lost. My 13th Para Battalion was alerted to support the 12th if need be. The Commando unit then rejoined its own Brigade.

While all this was going on an amusing incident occurred. Two German gunboats came up the canal from Ouistreham. Fire was held until they were close to the bridge; then one of them was put out of action by a PIAT fired by one of Howard's men close to the bridge and the men taken prisoner. The second boat turned in time and made off downstream.

And so the day passed. The pressure on the 7th and 12th Battalions never ceased. Sometimes the Germans succeeded in surrounding companies but they were always forced to withdraw.

At about 7pm the 2 I/C of 'A' Company of the 7th Battalion appeared at Pine-Coffin's HQ and gave the first full account the CO had had of the Company's doings. The Company Commander, Major Taylor, was a stretcher case. He had continued to command his Company and encourage his men propped up in a slit trench, but had then had to be evacuated. The Second-in-Command, Webber was also wounded, but carried on until he was evacuated to the UK that evening. The other officers were all casualties, one killed, another wounded but carrying on, and one missing since the drop. A counter-attack was urgently needed to enable the wounded to be collected and the Company to regroup.

The CO attempted a counter-attack with the small force he had assembled, replacing it temporarily with a platoon from Howard's Company. The attack, however, was not in sufficient strength to affect the enemy dispositions, but it served to reinforce 'A' Company. Howard's platoon was then returned to its reserve position between the bridges.

'A' Company had been fighting without pause since the early hours of the morning against superior numbers, supported by tanks and one SP gun, and inflicted heavy casualties on the enemy. They were tired and weakened by casualties but in good heart.

The fighting spirit in the 7th Battalion was equally reflected in Johnston's 12th Battalion. Relief came to the 12th in the evening when the 6th Airlanding Brigade landed by glider. The 248 gliders which carried this Brigade started landing on the Ranville dropping zone and a landing zone west of the canal just before 9pm. The whole Brigade landed in just half an hour. They hurried to the assistance of the 12th and put an end to what had been a most anxious day for this unit.

At about 10 pm the Royal Warwicks of the 3rd Division, from the seaborne landings, reached the bridges in strength and the relief of the 7th could begin. It was only completed just before midnight on 6/7 June, and a counter-attack had to be mounted to extract 'A' Company of the 7th who had fought so gallantly since early morning. When they and John Howard's company finally crossed the canal bridge late that night they were very exhausted soldiers, but they had every reason to be proud of themselves. Howard's spectacularly successful *coup de main* and the 7th, weak in numbers, like the 12th, but also, like them, not short of courage, had been hotly engaged, without pause, for some 21 hours and had repulsed all efforts of the Germans to dislodge them. The casualties to the Parachute Battalions had been heavy.

D-Day was over, but only to give place, for all these airborne men, to many days of heavy fighting.

Meanwhile, Brigadier Hill's 3rd Parachute Brigade had been

badly dropped. They were put down far to the east of their planned DZ. As a result, he and many of his men had been landed in the inundated area of the River Dives, from which they had great difficulty in extricating themselves. A large number of men were drowned in the swamps. Under the splendid leadership of Hill, in spite of his having been badly wounded at an early stage, his 8th and Canadian Battalions had by noon on D-Day reached the positions they were to hold on the ridge overlooking the Ranville and Benouville bridgehead. On the way the 8th and Canadian Parachute Battalions, with the support of the 3rd Parachute Squadron Royal Engineers, had successfully destroyed the bridges over the River Dives.

Brigadier Hill's 9th Para Battalion, which had also been badly dropped, were able to assemble only 150 of their men out of a total strength of 600. The Commanding Officer, Colonel Terence Otway, after waiting as long as he thought wise, decided to go ahead with his plans, in spite of his reduced numbers. They successfully assaulted the strongly defended Merville Battery and silenced the guns during the critical hours of the seaborne landings.

Thus, by midday on 6 June, all the tasks set to the 6th Airborne Division had been successfully accomplished.

Some may wonder what followed these exciting D-Day events. There was an important gap in the positions held by the 3rd Para Brigade and the Commando Brigade at Breville. This gap posed a serious threat to the Ranville-Benouville bridgehead and it was closed after a fierce battle at Breville on 12 June by 12th Para Battalion of my Brigade, together with a Company of the Devons and other Divisional troops under command of the 6th Airlanding Brigade.

Then there was a period of heavy fighting throughout the Normandy battlefront to establish the beachhead in depth and allow Monty to gain the city of Caen and group his allied forces for the wheel to the south and east and advance towards Paris and the Seine. This was the beginning of a move that later trapped so many German formations in the Falaise Gap.

Throughout this period the 6th Airborne Division held the Allied left flank firm. Then, when the general advance started, the Division led the way on that flank.

CHAPTER XIV

Putot and Pont L'Evêque

On 17 August the 6th Airborne Division had begun its breakout of the Normandy bridgehead. General Gale's advance was to be on the axis of the Route Nationale 175 and directed on the towns of Dozulé, Pont L'Evêque and Pont Audemer.

Brigadier Hill's 3rd Para Brigade was in the lead, on the right of the Division, and the 6th Airlanding Brigade were to make for Cabourg on the left. My 5th Para Brigade was in reserve, ready to exploit when the time came.

The advance eastward by the Division would involve a number of major river crossings. First the River Dives and valley, which the Germans had inundated extensively, making the country exceedingly difficult to cross. These inundations extended from Troarn in the west, to Dozulé in the east, and as far north as Cabourg.

East of the Dives Valley came the River Touques, which reaches the sea at Deauville, having passed through the considerable town of Pont L'Evêque. Then the River Risle, passing through Pont Audemer on its way to join the mouth of the Seine.

The ground on the east side of the Dives Valley rose steeply to the heights of Putot and Dozulé. At Troarn the valley was some 8000 yards across, bounded by the River Dives in the west and the Dives canal in the east. It was a formidable obstacle.

The 3rd Brigade made good progress in their advance as far as Goustranville, but in that town they were held by strong enemy resistance, including artillery fire, from the high ground at Putot. It was clear to Brigadier Hill that a daylight advance under observed enemy artillery fire would be very costly.

Accordingly, on the evening of 18 August, General Gale decided to put in a two-brigade night attack, with the object of forcing the crossing places of the Dives canal and then securing the high ground east of Putot. The enemy possession of that ground would endanger an advance by the Division along its main axis.

The night attack was to be a leapfrog, the 5th Para Brigade passing through the 3rd Brigade, when that Brigade had secured the line of the railway east of the canal. This railway line would then become the start line for the 5th Para Brigade attack. It was realized by General Gale and all of us that this was an ambitious and difficult task for my Brigade, but the General judged that it would be impossible for him to remain where he was, with enemy observation over his Division, then spread out in the open country, which was commanded from the heights of Putot.

In the sector in which Hill's attack was to take place there were four bridges over the Dives canal. In the north there was a bridge carrying the railway; some 500 yards to the south there was a smaller bridge; next there came the bridge carrying the Route Nationale 175 over the canal, and finally a much smaller bridge in the vicinity of a farm at Londes.

Hill's first task was to discover which, if any, of these bridges was intact. He was then to advance as far east as the railway and secure this as a start line for my attack on Putot.

Hill had decided that it would not be possible to start his advance before 10 pm. It was hoped that he would secure the railway, which was to be my start line, by 2.00 am. This would give me, at the best, only three hours of darkness during which to secure my objective — the Heights of Putot. The time was very short; I would not be able to make any firm plan or issue orders until it was known at which bridge Hill's crossing would be made and whether he had been successful in securing the start line for my attack.

It was going to be a difficult night!

I brought my Brigade forward at once to various concealed positions close to the village of Goustranville and from the church tower showed my Battalion Commanders as much as possible of the ground and gave them my general thinking on a plan for the night attack.

Hill's advance started punctually at 10 pm, and by 11 o'clock he had reached the canal. He then reported that the railway bridge in the north had been blown, but he thought it passable for infantry. The next bridge to the south was destroyed and the bridge carrying the Route Nationale had also been destroyed. There was no information yet on the farm bridge.

Hill decided to accept the damage to the northern railway bridge and he ordered the 9th Battalion to cross at once. They were then to turn south to secure my start line.

The crossing of the railway bridge proved much more difficult than expected. It was a lengthy business in the dark. The tide had raised the level of the canal and the men had to wade in a depth of something like three feet of water, a considerable hazard for the smaller men in the Battalion. It was, therefore, about 1.00 am before Hill's 9th Battalion was over and ready to move to the south.

At that time it was thought by Hill that the railway bridge was the only practicable crossing place and I accordingly directed the 13th Battalion, under Colonel Luard, to make for that bridge. At that time they were still at Goustranville. The Battalion was then to move behind the 9th Battalion to what would be my start line for the attack on Putot.

The route for the 13th Battalion to the railway bridge was difficult to follow because of the darkness and the many small watercourses to be crossed. By the time Luard reached the bridge the water level had risen still further and it was obvious that a crossing at that bridge was no longer possible.

In the meantime, the Canadian Parachute Battalion patrols had located a second small farm bridge close to the known one. These two narrow bridges thus became the only crossing places for the whole of my Brigade. There was now no alternative but to order the return of Luard's Battalion, through the same difficult route he had taken earlier, with a view to him making use of the farm bridges. The Battalion's return was led by the Commanding Officer whose experience as a skilled yachtsman was a great help. They reached the farm crossings in good order and remained there in reserve for the time being.

I was now able to finalize a plan for an attack by the Brigade on the Putot position. Colonel Pine-Coffin's 7th Battalion was to secure the spur immediately east of Putot, while Colonel Stockwell's 12th Battalion was to secure and mop up the village. The 12th Battalion attack was to start as soon as the 7th Battalion was in position. The 7th Battalion, however, had considerable difficulty, after crossing the canal, in reaching their start line for the attack on the spur east of Putot. The ground between the canal and their start line had not been completely mopped up and there was still a large number of enemy posts and anti-tank guns which had to be dealt with before the 7th Battalion could reach their start line.

During the move of the 7th Battalion a curious incident occurred. A party of about fifty Germans had not seen the 7th Battalion, as they lay concealed behind a hedge. The 7th was able to ambush them, causing heavy casualties, and could now move to their forming-up position and the 12th's assault on Putot began.

The church and cemetery of Putot stand on a very prominent mound which dominates the countryside in three directions. The ground at the bottom of the mound is, however, 'dead' ground for enemy in the village attempting to fire on the troops waiting to attack. The 12th then scaled the mound and pressed forward their attack with the greatest vigour in close hand-to-hand fighting. The German garrison of Putot were soon taken prisoner or killed.

The mopping-up of the village began and I moved my advanced Headquarters into the Manoir, a charming 17th century building. Unfortunately, this building soon became a target for German shelling!

Soon after we had seized Putot I learnt with great sadness that my jeep driver, Corporal Leatherbarrow, who had been with me throughout the Normandy Campaign and whom I had left in my jeep on the outskirts of the village, had been killed by a stray shell. It was a sad blow as Corporal Leatherbarrow had become a close friend.

As soon as the 12th had completed the mopping up of Putot, I ordered the 13th forward to secure first the spur running north from Putot, which had been the Brigade's original objective, and then to exploit eastwards and seize the high ground which overlooked Dozulé. Luard's first objective was strongly held but he secured it after a hard fight. When it came to exploiting towards the heights overlooking Dozulé, he met much stiffer opposition and could make no progress. Luard was suffering considerable casualties and I reached the conclusion that the task was beyond his resources in daylight and I ordered him to consolidate on the Brigade's original objective.

I then had a message from General Gale that he intended using the 4th Commando Brigade to put in a night attack on the high ground.

The achievement in seizing the heights above Putot-en-Auge

is best summarized in General Gale's own words as recorded in his book, *With the 6th Airborne Division in Normandy*:

This concluded the Putot-en-Auge Battle. It had proved a highly successful operation for the 5th Parachute Brigade. A night attack had been launched from a start line which had to be secured by a preliminary operation by another Brigade. The route to the start line had been uncertain until the last minute. Information regarding the crossing places of the Canal proved inaccurate and considerable adjustments in the plan had been necessary, these as late as 1.30 am. The route to the start had not been completely mopped up, and some opposition had been encountered on it by the leading Battalion, yet the final objective set to the Brigade was secured, though the further exploitation hoped for proved beyond their capacity.

The fighting spirit of the troops was splendid. They had no sleep during the night 18-19 August and had been up since 2 am the previous day, yet throughout the day their dash and energy never diminished, and in the evening the troops were in tremendous heart and well satisfied with their performance.

★   ★   ★

The task of the Brigade for 22 August was to secure the town of Pont L'Evêque and establish a bridgehead over the River Touques.

My orders were that the 13th Battalion was to advance on the axis of the Route Nationale 175 and infiltrate into the town. The 12th was to force a crossing south of the town and secure the St Julien feature which controlled the approach from the south. The Brigade reached the outskirts of the town at about 10 am. As soon as I arrived I reconnoitred the approaches to the St Julien feature which dominated the approach from the south and west. I concluded that an assault across the open ground south of the town, which was commanded from the high ground east of the river, would be too hazardous an operation in daylight. Accordingly I issued orders for a night attack. Recce patrols were sent out to prepare for this attack.

I then left for my HQ. En route I was intercepted by Colonel

Harvey with a personal message from the General. General Gale had been told by local people that the Germans were about to pull out of their town. Sensing the opportunity of cutting off their retreat, he sent orders, through Harvey, that the 'crossing was to be forced immediately in daylight and at all cost'. I returned at once and issued orders accordingly. Unfortunately the local information proved to be incorrect. The Germans were in fact preparing their defences for a stubborn battle.

Colonel Stockwell's plan for a daylight attack followed closely that which he had prepared for a night operation. He was to have the support of a regiment of artillery which would provide 20 minutes' smoke to help him over the open ground. He decided that his Battalion should advance on a one-company front. The second Company should move forward as soon as the first had crossed the open ground west of the river. Local guides had agreed to accompany the leading troops to identify the fords which were known to exist.

The attack started at 3 pm. The advance was in perfect order and the men were as steady as for a demonstration. All seemed to be going well and some men were seen to have crossed the river. Colonel Stockwell then ordered the second Company forward.

In fact the ford had not been found. Only the Company Commander, Captain Baker, and nine men had succeeded in getting across by swimming and these soon became casualties or were pinned down.

The second Company was also pinned down, along with the leading Company, by withering automatic fire and by shelling from the St Julien feature and the high ground east of the river. I realized that there was no prospect of success in daylight and that to go ahead would only result in unacceptable casualties. I therefore ordered the attack to cease and the Battalion to consolidate on the positions reached. The situation would be reviewed when it became dark.

I then went to the 13th Battalion in Pont L'Evêque to see how they had fared. The Battalion had had an initial success in penetrating into the town, but was now meeting increasingly severe opposition from well-sited and strongly defended German positions. Their advance was also greatly hampered by fires started by the Germans in many of the old wooden houses, a feature of the town. The Battalion had to fight their way forward yard by yard. They succeeded in crossing a secondary branch of the River Touques which separates from the main river south of the town.

A troop of tanks was brought forward but the tanks could not cross the secondary branch of the river until a crossing place had been prepared. The tanks then went forward to the vicinity of the church and were able to give useful covering fire. The tanks were, however, in a very vulnerable position; one of them was soon on fire and it was decided that they should be withdrawn.

The town was now burning fiercely and, after a reconnaissance with Colonel Luard, I decided that it would not be practicable to make a further attempt to force the crossing of the main river until the fires in the town had died down. At this stage it was thought that the only means of crossing the main river was by the girder (Fig. 5) and that was under constant fire. I accordingly ordered Colonel Luard to consolidate in the positions reached.

I then asked for a meeting with the Divisional Commander to discuss the situation. The General sent his GSO1 forward to Brigade HQ where he met me. It was agreed that no further attack should be pressed by Colonel Luard that night and that his Battalion should be ready to seize a crossing place in the morning if this appeared possible. It was also agreed that the proposed attack on the St Julien feature during the night should be cancelled. It was further agreed that, after dark, the 12th Battalion should withdraw from its unpleasant position south of the town. It would then come into reserve and the 7th Battalion assume responsibility for the west and south approaches to the town. Fortunately the night proved relatively quiet. The Brigade casualties on 22 August had been thirty-four killed and sixty-one wounded. The Germans had suffered much more heavily. Local people reported 127 new German graves and ambulances busy all night evacuating wounded.

In the morning Colonel Luard and I carried out a recce. A patrol under Captain Skeate had succeeded in crossing the river without opposition, the fires in the burning town had died down somewhat and it appeared that the chance of securing a bridgehead on the far bank was now favourable. I therefore ordered Colonel Luard to secure this bridgehead with the utmost speed.

'B' Company was soon across and attempted to increase the foothold gained by Skeate's patrol, but then met stiff resistance and were held up. Major Cramphorne's Company came to their assistance, but the Germans were well established in good

79

positions and every yard was stiffly fought. At noon it was reported by Major Ford, the Second-in-Command, that both Companies were held up and that the Germans were attempting to infiltrate between their positions.

It was clear to me that the foothold gained by the 13th Battalion on the east bank of the river was too small and the communications too insecure to make it practicable as a route for a fresh attack. Its retention could only lead to severe casualties. I therefore decided to withdraw the 13th Battalion and that the 7th Battalion should assume responsibility for the western end of the town, and form a firm base through which the 13th Battalion could withdraw.

The withdrawal was skilfully conducted and was carried out in a most gallant and steady manner. It was thought that the iron girder was the only means of crossing the river. It was, however, under continual fire. Fortunately, it was discovered that, by using a rope, it was possible to wade the river at one place. After passing through the 7th Battalion, the 13th came into Reserve. The casualties during the morning had been twelve killed and thirty-three wounded.

The night of the 23/24 August was quiet. Patrols at first light, 6 am, discovered that the Germans had slipped out of the town during the night. I ordered an immediate follow-up by the 7th Battalion on the axis of the Pont Audemer road. At 10 am the General arrived at Brigade HQ. He gave orders for an immediate advance on Pont Audemer. The 7th Battalion had already got well beyond the first of the Division's bounds and their progress fitted in well with the Divisional plan. During this visit the General placed the Armoured Reconnaissance Regiment and the Royal Netherlands Brigade under my command.

At last the charming and historic town of Pont L'Evêque had been liberated. The fierceness of the earlier fighting between the 13th Battalion and the German defenders, lasting some two and a half days, can be judged by the sad destruction of houses throughout the town and of the fine church of St Michel. The blazing town had added to the horror of the battle for soldiers and civilians.

The 7th Para Battalion, in spite of a most exhausting few days, showed their toughness and marching qualities by the speed at which they reached Pont Audemer and secured the west bank of the River Risle. They reached the town at almost the same time as the motorized units of the Dutch Brigade and the Armoured Recce Regiment. The 7th Battalion was relieved the next day by the 49th Division.

The final dash to Pont Audemer marked the end of our Normandy campaign. A message had come to General Gale saying that the 6th Airborne Division would be withdrawn from the line and sent back to England as soon as shipping could be provided.

Complimentary messages came from the Army Commander and Corps Commander giving their 'immense appreciation' for the contribution made by the Division during the advance from the Normandy Bridgehead.

We were now to be sent to England to prepare for an operation elsewhere. We embussed in vehicles in the Trouville area and then set off for Arromanches from where we would embark. This proved a most uncomfortable procedure as the sea was rough and we had to climb up the side of our ships using scrambling nets. Fortunately we had only one serious accident.

Back at home, we had a kind welcome from everyone at Bulford and Larkhill, where we were based, and then went on a short period of leave. It was splendid to see our families again. Julia was at our Old Green Lane house at Camberley with the family, consisting now of three children. It was a short but happy leave.

CHAPTER XV

The Division Fights On

We did not have long to wait for another assignment. It was in December, 1944, that von Rundstedt's massive assault burst into the American sector of the Ardennes. The Americans gave way and the Battle of the Bulge began. The 6th Airborne Division was available and we were hurriedly despatched to the Ardennes by road and sea to fill the gap. The German effort was halted and pursuit became the order of the day. The 13th Battalion played a gallant part, but at the cost of heavy casualties.

When the situation in the Ardennes was under control, the Division was sent to Holland where we held a section of the River Maas. During our short time there, we were in close contact with the Germans night and day, on the opposite bank, and we became fine boatmen.

Now we were called home again to prepare for the final great battle of the war — the crossing of the Rhine on 24 March, 1945.

A massive force of Allied troops, under Field-Marshal Montgomery, had been assembled on the west bank of the Rhine in readiness for the assault. The crossing began during the early morning of the 24th using assault landing craft.

Then, at 10 am, the Airborne Corps under the command of the US General Matthew Ridgway, and comprising our 6th Airborne Division and the US 17th Airborne Division, were to drop simultaneously, in broad daylight, on top of the German defenders on the east bank of the river and on their gun positions. Now we would be up against high-quality German troops, a number of which were parachute units. Our task was to extend the depth of the bridgehead which was to be secured by the waterborne assault and enable the allied force to achieve a rapid build-up on the east bank in readiness for an advance across the Hanoverian Plain.

As the waterborne assault was to start early in the morning, there could be no surprise for this vast airborne landing. The whole force of Allied airborne troops was to fly in a single lift. This would consist of 540 US Dakota aircraft carrying twelve Allied battalions of parachute troops flying wing-tip to wing-tip and followed by 1,300 gliders which would land the British and American gliderborne units. The operation would be supported by some 10,000 aircraft. Winston Churchill, in spite of Field-Marshal Montgomery's protest, insisted in watching this great air armada from a position close to the forward troops.

Our two British Parachute Brigades, James Hill's 3rd Brigade and my own 5th Brigade, had assembled in transit camps in East Anglia and moved to the airfields from which we would fly during the early hours of the morning. There we emplaned. We took off at 7 in the morning. The Dakota aircraft were vastly more comfortable than the aircraft we had used for Normandy, Albemarles and Stirlings, and much easier to jump from.

It was a beautiful clear day and we had a magnificent view as the formations of our transport aircraft crossed the channel between Folkestone and Cap Gris Nez and linked up just south of Brussels with our American counterpart carrying the 17th US Airborne Division. Then the 450 parachute aircraft passed below the glider stream as they flew on, protected by its fighter cover. This was a sight that none of us who took part will forget. As we approached the Rhine we could see ahead the battlefield, covered by the haze and the dust of the bombardment. At 1,000 feet we could see the area of the army administrative units and the supporting arms and artillery as we flew on, and so on to the crossing places themselves.

There was no time to interest ourselves in the troops on the ground or in the craft on the river. The red light − 'prepare to jump' − was on and, almost before we realized that we were over enemy territory, we were being shot at ourselves and the aircraft bumped and shook. We were over the DZ, the green light was on and we were out, dangling from our parachutes and trying in the very short time available to identify the landmarks which had seemed so clear and simple on the sand model and photographs, but looked so different as we came down rapidly into the firing and the smoke and the dust that had been left by the preliminary bombardment.

The bombardment had finished 10 minutes before we landed

and, heavy as it had been, there was ample time for those German defences not knocked out to recover their balance sufficiently to be a considerable menace to the parachutist, as we swung in the air or disentangled ourselves from our parachutes and searched for our bearings. Those who had fallen in trees were unluckiest and many became casualties to German automatic fire. We all felt very naked.

This is where the battle experience of the Brigade told. Assembly to the individual unit RVs is a tricky business with a concentrated drop of men of different units, inevitably mixed up. We had all been shot at on the way down and, on the ground, there was considerable harassing fire. Men were struggling to get out of their parachutes and undo their kitbags, in which their weapons were carried. At the same time we were trying to recognise the landmarks to our various rendezvous.

Although we had been well dropped, individual officers and men had difficulty in picking up their exact positions. This period on the DZ was where most of our casualties occurred. Once an enemy position had been located and action taken to deal with it, the enemy often surrendered without a hard fight. Until they had been located, these posts were a serious menace.

Just as the parachutists were reaching their RVs the glider element of the Brigade Group began to land in front of us and others to the south. These landings caused a considerable diversion of the fire away from us, but it was a tragic sight for us to see our gliders being hit and often blown up. The losses among the gliders were very heavy and only a small proportion of the anti-tank guns and vehicles carrying machine guns reached us. If a strong enemy counter-attack had come that afternoon we should have had a difficult time.

It was about one hour after the drop that battalions were sufficiently complete in their RVs for us to start the offensive action phase of our plan.

Considering the circumstances of the landing, casualties to the parachutists were no higher than we expected. They were about 20% of those who jumped or landed by glider, but some important key personnel were missing. I lost my Brigade Major and my Signals Officer on the DZ and my Chief Administrative Officer, Ted Lough, in a glider. He was very badly wounded. Lough was a sad loss, both as a personal friend and a key man.

The Battle of the Rhine had gone well throughout the front

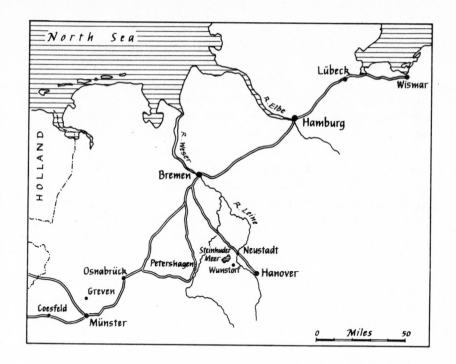

and the 1st Corps was ready to move forward earlier than expected. By the evening of 26 March my Brigade was established some two miles east of the River Ijssel and Hamminkeln and we received orders to advance at once on the town of Erle.

As we moved forward the German resistance stiffened. We made our advance into the town by night and attacked it from the rear. We achieved complete surprise and captured about 200 prisoners.

This type of encirclement operation became a pattern for most of our operations and was highly successful. The important thing was to keep up the momentum of our advance and not allow the Germans time to withdraw in an orderly manner and reform. At this stage all movement was on foot.

Morale was high and long distances were covered, knowing that in this way casualties could be kept to a minimum. Fifty miles were covered on foot during the first three days. This included two night attacks and almost continuous fighting or marching. It was a tremendous achievement and the troops had every reason to be proud of themselves.

At this stage a squadron of Grenadiers from Lieutenant-Colonel Charlie Tryon's Armoured Regiment joined us. It was a great help. We also began to get some lorries which speeded up our movement. And thus the advance went on; Coesfeld, then Greven and next Osnabruck became our objectives, always using much the same tactics, which were proving so successful. We secured a footing in Osnabruck during the night and then, when it was light enough, pushed on into the town to seize the main features and mop up.

Next we were making for Petershagen and then Neustadt. At Wunstorf an important bridge was seized intact after a gallant action by Ken Darling and his 12th Battalion. Meanwhile the 7th Battalion, under Geoffrey Pine-Coffin, had seized the bridge at Neustadt. Peter Luard's 13th Battalion was then directed on to Steinhuder and the 7th Battalion on to Wunstorf airfield.

We were now reaching the Leine River where the bridge was seized intact and a bridgehead for another bridge was secured.

At this stage the 6th Airborne Division was ordered, to their great disappointment, to halt and allow the 15th Scottish Division to pass through. We regarded this as quite unnecessary; we were fit and anxious to go on. A delay of three or four days was involved in passing the 15th Scottish through. This slowed up the whole advance and resulted in considerable casualties to their Division. The momentum of the advance having been lost, the 15th Scottish were again held up on the River Elbe and we passed through them there.

We then made at all possible speed for the Baltic with Wismar as the goal. It was here that we met the Russians. Fraternization was the order from higher command and we visited one another's headquarters and had a meal together. It was here that Monty came to our Divisional Headquarters to meet the Russian Commander, General Rokossovsky. Some of us were present at the meeting. Monty was very agreeable and complimentary about the Division.

In no time it was VE Day. One of my companies was sent to Copenhagen to occupy the airfield and I took the opportunity of visiting them.

A few days later we were ordered back to the UK. We had moved so fast during the advance that we had ended in the zone allocated to the Russian occupation forces.

And so for us the European campaign was over. The war in Europe had been won. We felt proud to have played our part.

CHAPTER XVI

The 5th Parachute Brigade
in South-East Asia

The story of the 6th Airborne Division on D-Day has been well told by many of those who took part. Perhaps not so many know of the adventures, following VE Day, of the 5th Parachute Brigade in South-East Asia.

After the Rhine Crossing and the Division's gallop through Germany and their contact with the Russians at Wismar on the Baltic and to the South, we celebrated VE Day, and then the Division returned to the UK and leave. Many thought that the war for us was over.

I was enjoying my leave fishing on the Tweed when a telephone message came from the house asking that a car be sent to meet a light aircraft which would be landing shortly in a field nearby. It would bring a letter for me. The aircraft touched down and out got John Wrightson of the Divisional staff. The letter said that I was to return immediately to Bulford. My Brigade was under orders for South-East Asia. We were to play our part in the war against Japan.

It was sad for our wives and families that we should be leaving again so soon, but that is the life of a soldier.

I was to leave as soon as possible, by flying-boat. General Bols, the Divisional Commander, and two of his staff would come with us. We were to go first to Kandy in Ceylon, the Headquarters of the Supreme Allied Commander, Admiral Mountbatten. At that time General 'Boy' Browning was the Admiral's Chief of Staff and he made us very welcome.

I soon learnt from the General that my task would be a parachute landing to seize the causeway between Singapore Island and the mainland of Malaya. It was part of the operation, codenamed 'Zipper', to regain the Malayan Peninsula. I had amusing discussions with General Browning on possible dropping zones; he fan-

9 Princess Alexandra accepts the badge of the Durham Light Infantry on her appointment as Colonel-in-Chief, 17 May, 1958 (see p.128).

10 "On each of these visits the Ambassador took me to see President Diem" (p.140). On the left is Mr. Harry Hohler, the British Ambassador, on the right Colonel Henry Lee, the Military Attaché.

11 Visiting Korea when Commander-in-Chief, United Kingdom Far East Land Forces. The author with General G.S. Meloy, Jr., Commander-in-Chief, United Nations Command, Korea (see p.146).

12 The author with the Rt. Hon. Keith Holyoake, Prime Minister of New Zealand and the Hon. D.J. Eyre, Minister of Defence, 6 March, 1962 (see p.151).

cied a pineapple plantation. Such a prickly landing did not appeal to me! As the best of a bad lot, I preferred young rubber. General Bols and his party went home after a couple of days. It was clear that there was no role for the rest of the Division in 'Zipper'.

I still had work to do with the operational and intelligence staffs, but, after about a week, moved to Bombay to prepare for the arrival of my Brigade. The Chief Justice's house had been turned into a Senior Officers' Mess. We were very comfortable, but there was sometimes feeling about the allotment of accommodation. The Mess Secretary did not understand the important difference between a Naval and an Army Captain! Feelings were hurt.

My Brigade Group arrived during July and we at once set about strenuous training, but we had to be careful of the hot and sticky climate. Then came the time for planning. We would not be concerned in the initial assault, but would land when a beachhead had been secured.

In mid-August, just as were about to embark, the atom bomb was dropped. 'Zipper', as planned, was cancelled. Nonetheless we embarked on our troopship and set sail for Malaya. The revised plan involved a landing, from landing craft, on the Morib beaches in Malaya. We were expecting a nice sandy beach, but instead were often above our knees in sticky mud. All went well, however, and the leading elements of the Brigade Group were soon ashore. We did not know what reception we would get from the local people. We knew that the communists had gained a strong footing throughout Malaya and that we could take no chances.

Following our instructions, the first troops to land set off on the route to Kuala Lumpur, passing, at frequent intervals, arches with communist slogans and the title Anti-Japanese People's Army.

We made good progress on our way and then received a message to say that Kuala Lumpur was in our hands and that we were to make for Singapore. 'Transport' would be provided.

Soon after our arrival at Singapore, I went to see General Dempsey, C-in-C Allied Land Forces. He had known us well in Normandy days. He told me exactly what he wanted us to do. First on his list was to help the Police. Their organization had been broken up by the Japanese and their best men had disappeared. There were few British officers or junior ranks. The help we could give was mostly in man-management, discipline and organization.

As regards our own men, it was a tricky time throughout South-East Asia. The men's thoughts were on home. Their morale and contentment were of top importance. They needed plenty of occupation and as much sport as possible. Our work with the Police, perhaps, helped us as much as them.

Early in December it was decided that we were to go to Batavia, now known as Djakarta. In August, 1945, before the arrival of the British, Sukarno had made a Declaration of Independence and named himself President. He had a large following of politicians and armed extremists supporting him, and there were disturbances in many parts of the country. The Dutch, on the other hand, wanted to put the clock back to pre-war days. Neither of these courses was acceptable, at that time, to HMG.

In December, 1945, when my Brigade reached Batavia, the town was already firmly in British hands. There was, however, still serious fighting in the outskirts of Semarang and Surabaya. No operational role had been allotted to the Brigade in Batavia. Units from the European theatre were perhaps not popular with those which had fought through the Burma Campaign.

The policy to finish the war in Europe first and concentrate our military resources to that end must have been very frustrating to the Burma Army. It was not a happy atmosphere.

Something needed to be done. I asked the General at Batavia for an operational role which would stretch our capabilities. A certain amount of regrouping was going on and it was decided that we should go to Semarang to relieve the troops there, who would then rejoin their parent formation. This was a perfect solution for us.

Semarang would be an independent Command. In addition to my Brigade Group I would have a troop of tanks and a troop of Field Artillery. Also, interestingly, a Battalion Group of Japanese, some 500 strong. The unit under Major Kido had behaved outstandingly well during a battle in Semarang in October, 1945. They had defeated a well-armed force of some 3,000 Indonesians and rescued a large number of Dutch, locked in the gaol and whom it was thought might be murdered. As a result Kido's unit had been allowed to retain their weapons and become part of the force defending Semarang.

Before leaving Batavia I was approached by a group of former

Dutch officials who wished to take over the civil administration of the Semarang District. I could foresee a host of problems and I reassured them, politely, that my Brigade Group would be capable of undertaking any civil task that might come its way, such as clearing up the town after the devastation of fighting, checking on the medical arrangements, restoring the water supply, repairing the roads and the drainage. The Dutch were followed by Mr Sphirir who was said to be Prime Minister of Sukarno's Government. He appealed to me in the same terms as the Dutch. My answer was the same. I would look after the civil and military affairs in Semarang.

Our first task, on arrival, was to review the defensive layout and ensure that the key positions, such as the Gombel Hill feature, Tjandi and the airstrip, on which our communications and supplies depended, were secure.

The Brigade soon settled in. They were thrilled once more to have a job of importance. Their tails were sky high. There were nightly patrols to ensure that the well-armed Indonesian forces did not mount a surprise attack or infiltrate into our positions.

When going round the units in the morning, it seemed strange to be visiting the Japanese whom we treated in exactly the same way as our own people. They were efficient and co-operative.

We soon established friendly relations with the Dutch and Indonesians in the town and also the Chinese. We made good progress in tidying up the town. Our Royal Engineers, with local help, got the water supply and electricity functioning. Our Field Ambulance helped with hospital and medical arrangements. We soon had an efficient police force operating. We received grateful thanks from the local population for this, particularly from the Chinese. All this time the battalions were pressing on with their military training. The units were close together and there was a healthy spirit of competition.

General Dempsey, at that time C-in-C Allied Land Forces, came to visit us. He had known us well in Normandy and again in Singapore and he went round all my units. He saw them on parade and he talked to many of the men. He wrote to me afterwards that he had never seen the Brigade in better shape, nor the men happier. He was delighted with them.

During this visit General Dempsey told me that he had had a personal telegram from the War Office asking that I should return to the UK as soon as possible to take up another appointment.

He had not been told what the appointment was, but he knew it was an important one, close to the CIGS, Sir Alan Brooke. We discussed my successor and a date for the handover and he invited me to stay at Flagstaff House, Singapore, while he was getting me on to an aircraft. My new appointment was in fact to be Director of Plans at the War Office. The General sent Julia a telegram to say that I would soon be coming home.

Then the time came for me to leave. I had formed the 5th Parachute Brigade during the summer of 1943 and had commanded them, throughout the successful Normandy campaign and afterwards, for close on three years. They were my friends, indeed, I felt, part of my family. It was a wrench to leave them. I had to say goodbye to Geoffrey Pine-Coffin, to Peter Luard and to many others, officers and men who had been with me from the start. It was hard to say goodbye and thank them enough. There were also goodbyes in Semarang to the local people, Dutch and Chinese, who had helped us so much. Also to the Japanese unit which had behaved in an exemplary manner. I had taken the opportunity of having a word with General Dempsey about the desirability of repatriating the Japanese as soon as practicable. They had been promised repatriation as a unit. I had detected no trouble, but it could blow up quickly and would be dangerous. I was glad to hear that before long they were sent back to Japan.

Then I was off. I was given a kind farewell by the troops of the Brigade Group, including the Japanese. The Brigade lined the road between my Headquarters and the airfield. It was a moving occasion.

I handed over Command to Brigadier Ken Darling on 15 February, 1946.

CHAPTER XVII

Director of Plans at the War Office

I was delighted to be given a key post at the War Office, particularly as I was new to the Operations and Plans Directorate. The Planning Staff was also, collectively, the Staff of the Chiefs of Staff Committee, and I would, therefore, be brought into close contact with that Committee, which handled important matters of inter-service and Government defence policy.

When I took over as D of P Lord Alanbrooke was CIGS and, as the longest-serving member of the Chief's of Staff Committee, he was also the Chairman of that Committee. He was a brilliant Chairman and, in spite of the problems that arose between the Chiefs over the allocation of funds between the three services, during a period of acute financial crisis, he was able to maintain the confidence and support of his colleagues, neither of whom were easy. Lord Tedder was the Chief of the Air Staff and Sir John Cunningham First Sea Lord.

During Lord Alanbrooke's period the Directors of Plans of the three services attended the Chiefs of Staff (COS) meetings. This was a great help to us. We heard their discussion before they gave us their directions on the subjects they wished studied and thus we knew their thoughts on these.

On 1 July Lord Alanbrooke retired and Monty took his place as CIGS. Lord Tedder then became Chairman of the COS Committee. Sir John Cunningham sat on Tedder's right. Monty did not like it at all.

The COS Committee then became a most unhappy organization. Monty and Tedder disliked each other intensely. Monty knew that, during the Normandy campaign, Tedder had intrigued against him and done his best to get him sacked. Sir John Cunningham was clever but he did not hit it off with Monty. It was well known that Monty disliked the committee system used by the COS. He reckoned that it led to 'woolly' thinking and lack

93

of decisive action. He was accustomed to a commander or chairman who, after discussion and decision, issued orders and saw that they were carried out. That system was unacceptable to the other two. There were constant rows in the COS Committee and a lot of jealousy over the position of national standing that Monty had acquired.

Because of the quarrels at the COS meetings, the D's of P were no longer allowed to attend throughout. We would wait in the anteroom until our papers were being considered and then we would be summoned. This made our work more difficult.

When Monty was appointed CIGS there was also a good deal of anxiety in the corridors of the War Office. He had never served in the War Office and it was generally thought that he did not think much of it. It seemed likely that he would introduce changes in organization and staff and generally stir things up! I must admit that I did not fancy my own chances of survival. Although I had met Monty on many occasions in Normandy, I knew that he had a first-class team of planners of his own, whom he knew well, and might wish to bring with him.

I was greatly relieved when I learnt that there would be no change in my Directorate. Monty was always very good to me. When I went to see him, as I did most days, he was very agreeable. We would sit round his table and discuss the papers which were to be considered by the COS and I would explain the reasons for any conclusions by the Directors of Plans which were perhaps questionable. I much enjoyed working for him and I believe that this was the experience of most of us who worked closely with him. Senior officers may not always have had such an easy passage. Those who had not played an active part in the war soon learnt that, as far as Monty was concerned, they were finished.

I spent eighteen happy months with Monty and, in spite of the problems that arose between him and his fellow Chiefs of Staff, I have nothing but happy recollections of working under him.

The work I was doing made it essential for me to live in London. The family were well established in a house we had rented in the part of the Avon Valley known as the Woodford Valley, some five miles north of Salisbury. Julia and the children and Nanny had lots of friends and Joanna had her pony in a field belonging to the house. We did not want to move.

Mrs Seary-Mercer, with whom I had P.G.'d during the war, had kindly offered me a room at 64 Cadogan Square which Julia could share when she could get to London and where I could have breakfast and dinner. In spite of the sadness of not being together during the week, we decided to accept that arrangement.

The Directors of Plans had one day a week off, a Saturday. We had meetings on Sundays, so that we could work at COS papers and be ready for the usual Chief's of Staff meeting on Monday.

In the meantime I was working hard to get on top of my job with the Joint Planning Staff. Jack Stevens was the Admiralty Director and George Mills was the Air Ministry Director. We all got on well together. A most important member of the Joint Planning Committee was our Foreign Office Representative. During most of my time we were lucky to have Harold Caccia. Later he became Lord Caccia, having served as Ambassador at Washington and head of the Foreign Service. Our Foreign Office Representative doubled that job with being Chairman of the Joint Intelligence Committee. As a member of the Foreign Office, he had access to all the Foreign Office branches and we were able to make use of their knowledge in our work. The Foreign Office link was invaluable to us. Shortly before I left, Caccia was replaced by William Hayter, another first-class brain, who later became HM Ambassador in Moscow.

The system used by the JP Committee had been developed between the two wars and well practised since. In general the Chiefs of Staff directed the Planners on the matters they wished studied. The Directors would then allocate work on the study to one of the inter-service teams. They would produce a draft paper with the assistance of their own Foreign Office Representative and could consult any other Government Department which might have an interest in the matter. During my time there was no Chairman appointed for the JP Committee. The Director most concerned with the subject would, in agreement with the others, probably take the chair. If there was no obvious Chairman, the matter would be settled easily between the three of us. The Chairman might even be the last Director to take his seat at a meeting.

An example of the sort of matter that came to the Joint Planning Committee was the anxiety, in London and Washington, over whether we were properly prepared if the political agreements made at the end of the war between the British, US and Russians were not adhered to. Discussions had taken place in London with the Americans and it was clearly necessary that the

C-in-C British Forces in Germany, at that time Marshal of the RAF Sir Sholto Douglas, should be informed of what had been going on in London and the conclusions of the Chiefs of Staff.

I was instructed to go to Germany and brief him. The Chiefs were aware that, as C-in-C in Germany, he would be more than surprised at not having been consulted at the outset. It was for security reasons, political as well as military, that the Chiefs had acted as they had.

The arrangement was that, on arrival in Germany, I should go first to the Army C-in-C, Sir Richard McCreery, and that he should take me to see Sir Sholto Douglas. At the outset the meeting was not a happy one. Sholto Douglas was indignant that the Chiefs had not consulted him earlier. I explained the political and military factors which had led the Chiefs to prefer the private briefing that I had come over to give. Sir Richard McCreery was a great help to me. After a certain amount of hard speaking, Sholto Douglas accepted the reasons for the Chiefs handling the matter themselves, but he was not pleased, and I undertook to pass on his views to the Chiefs of Staff. He then invited me to return in a fortnight and stay with him. He would then take me to Berlin where I would stay with him again, while he briefed his senior Commanders. What was always going to be a tricky assignment ended up agreeably.

In Berlin I was particularly pleased to met General Brownjohn. He had been my boss in 1940 at the War Office and, when he left on promotion, I had been promoted Lieutenant-Colonel to take his place. He arranged for me to see some of the sights of Berlin such as Hitler's Bunker. The destruction in Berlin was terrible to behold.

Towards the end of 1947 I was told that I had been selected for the Imperial Defence College course, starting in January, 1948. This was good news, although I was sorry to leave my job as Director of Plans.

A wag once christened the I.D.C. course as 'taking the broad view from 10 to 4'. It is true that the pressure of work was very different to my previous two years, but the object of this course was to broaden our outlook beyond the purely military field. Also there was great value in the way we were able to mix and make friends with officers of the other services and with civil servants, all of whom were likely to hold posts of importance in the future.

The Commandant while I was there was Air Chief Marshal Sir

John Slessor. He had a wide circle of friends in business and the academic world as well as in the services and was able to call upon a splendid team of speakers on a wide variety of subjects. The practice was for the speaker of the day to talk for an hour or so, after which the subject would be open for general discussion, which would probably continue informally during lunch. Guests with something to contribute were encouraged.

The I.D.C. was in one of the fine corner houses in Belgrave Square, well set up and furnished. We found our own accommodation in London or not too far afield. I remained at 64 Cadogan Square.

Julia and I had decided that she should pay a visit to New Zealand at the end of 1947 so that she could see her family and they could see her and the children. This would mean a great deal to her parents who had suffered terribly during the war. They had lost three sons in the Air Force, one in the RAF and two in the RNZAF. In addition they had two sons serving in the Royal Navy, one commanding a destroyer, the other a submarine.

While Julia was in New Zealand I was enjoying my time at the I.D.C. The morning was given up to lectures and discussions and after lunch we might have syndicate meetings or study papers for some task we had been set.

An interesting feature of the course was a tour which we did during the summer. We were invited to choose from about four alternative tours. In my year we were offered the USA, Germany or the Far East. A possible India tour had to be cancelled because of the political situation there. We did not always get the tour chosen. I was allotted the German tour. This was sensible as I had not served there since the war. We went to Frankfurt, Bonn, Hanover and Hamburg. Excellent programmes were prepared for us in each place, the American zone being particularly interesting.

Before returning to London I went to visit some German relations. My mother was an American and one of her sisters had married a German before the First World War. My mother's sister was no longer alive, but I visited their family in their house not far from the Elbe. One of the cousins is now a General in the new German Army.

Towards the end of my year at the I.D.C. I was called away to take part in an important study on the shape and size of the armed forces. It was a period of great financial stringency and the Chiefs of Staff had been unable to agree on the allocation of funds between the three Services.

Eventually the Minister of Defence, A.V. Alexander, had directed that an independent study should be made and the Report given directly to him. The Harwood Committee, named after its Chairman, a civil servant, was set up to undertake the study. Harwood had been on the Directing Staff of the I.D.C. before my day. Admiral Lambe was the naval member. Later he became First Sea Lord. Air Marshal Ivelaw-Chapman, who had been on the Directing Staff of the I.D.C. with me, was the airman. I was the soldier, rather more junior than the others, but I had the experience of having been Director of Plans. Each of us was allowed one Staff Officer from his own service. He would be of Lieutenant-Colonel or equivalent rank.

We worked in considerable secrecy, in the wartime extension of the Admiralty, known as Lenin's Tomb. We were not allowed access to our own Ministries, nor were we to consult them. It was to be an independent Report with our own conclusions. Our Staff Officers were allowed into the Ministries to gather information and obtain costings, but not to consult.

Our terms of reference were to make recommendations on the 'shape and size' of the armed forces within a total budget ceiling of £700m. These terms amounted to asking us to recommend how that sum should best be spent for the benefit of national defence. We tried to be completely objective in our study and to forget that we belonged to any particular service.

We did all our work in one large room. Ivelaw-Chapman and I sat opposite one another at a large double desk. Charles Lambe sat opposite Harwood. This was a good arrangement as we could discuss things easily and informally.

Our first course was to look at our existing world strategy and commitments and judge how essential we felt that modern weapons and aircraft were under the current world conditions. Could all our commitments still be justified as essential? What was required to defend these commitments? If we were to keep within our budget figure, it would mean cutting out some major spenders. Paring off bits would be no good.

For example, was Bomber Command really essential in the world of tomorrow? (Remember that we were thinking of these matters more than 40 years ago.) Should the Royal Marines be a separate service or could they use the facilities and training establishments of the army? How significant would any possible savings be? These were dramatic questions we were asking ourselves. There were many more. I was on a rather easy wicket. Soldiers had to be readily available when a dangerous situation arose. Men were being killed in Palestine, they were being killed in the Middle East and in Malaya. If they had to be mobile they must have vehicles. They had to have the right weapons, as good or better than the enemy.

Our report was printed early in 1949. It was the best part of an inch thick and was duly delivered to the Minister with copies sent to the Service Ministries. Some of the proposals caused the alarm that we expected. The report also had the result which we hoped. It showed that £700m was not enough to meet the country's defence needs. Fresh terms of reference were then given to the Chiefs of Staff. They were to plan within a much larger budget. The conclusions and recommendations in our report were set out and costed in great detail and the report was made considerable use of by the Ministries in the years ahead.

Just before I left the I.D.C. in October, 1948, Monty had been appointed Chairman of the new Western Union Organization. At much the same time the Army students at the I.D.C. were told of their appointments when the course was finished. I would be going to Monty at the Western Union HQ. Shortly after that I had a letter from him from Switzerland saying how pleased he was that I was coming to him and that when he got back to England he would let me know how he wanted me to work. I had got on well with Monty and I was pleased to be asked to go back to him, but the job was not at all what I wanted. I had done my stint at the War Office and I now wanted to serve with soldiers in a field formation. I therefore got in touch with the Military Secretary and sought his help. Monty quite understood my position and agreed that I should go to a field formation when something suitable became available and my appointment with him was cancelled.

Although we had delivered our Harwood Committee Report, there was some supplementary work which the Chiefs wanted us to do before we were dispersed and so it was March before I was free.

Before I left the War Office Field-Marshal Slim sent for me and said that he was very pleased with the contribution I had made on the Harwood Committee and that he felt that the Army had been well looked after.

After the war finished in Europe, the British established a Military Mission in Greece to help the Greek Government against communist infiltration that was taking place on the northern frontier. We provided training teams with the Greek Army formations and a Directing Staff for their Staff College. The Headquarters of the Mission also acted in an advisory capacity for operations. At the beginning of 1949 financial problems in the UK caused the British Government to decide to discontinue the Military Mission. The Americans began to take over some of the earlier functions, but we still exercised a major influence over operations on the frontier and maintained close relations with Field-Marshal Papagos and other senior officers in the Greek Army.

The Commander of the Military Mission at this time was General Down. He had served in the Airborne Forces and we knew each other well. It was agreed that I should go out to Greece as his Deputy for a short time. The British members of the mission were in an advisory capacity and were to take no part in active operations, but I would travel over a large part of Greece and get to know the Greek Army and their generals and senior officers. The Government forces were at that time beginning to gain control of the frontier and victory was in sight. It was an interesting job.

I had a house allotted to me which had belonged to a shipping millionaire, Goulandris. It was well fitted out, with fine marble floors in all the rooms and a marble terrace and fountain outside the sitting room, looking out on the mountains.

A great asset in going round the Greek coast and islands was a large motor launch manned by an RASC crew which would sleep four people. I visited many Greek formations in this way.

When I reached Greece I was anxious that Julia should join me from New Zealand as soon as possible, as I knew she would enjoy it. She had the greatest difficulty in getting a passage and finally had to come out via the UK. She eventually reached me in August, bringing the three children with her.

Before long General Sir John Crocker, C-in-C Middle East, who had been our Corps Commander in Normandy, sent me a signal that he would like me to go to Fayid, his house in the Canal Zone, to stay with him for a few days. I had not been long with him before he told me that I was to be promoted to Major-General and to be Chief of Staff to General Harding, the C–in–C Far East Land Forces. I only knew General Harding by reputation but it would be no exaggeration to say that he was the best-loved General in the army.

We had a few more weeks in Athens to say goodbye to friends, British, Greek and American, and then set out for England. After a month's leave we were on our way to the Far East and the start of another appointment.

CHAPTER XVIII

With Sir John Harding in the Far East

While I was at the War Office in June, 1950, being briefed on events in the Far East, the Korean War broke out and our possible contribution was under discussion. This was something to add to an already disturbed situation. The Malayan Emergency was at its height, although, with John Harding as C-in-C, Roy Urquhart as GOC Malaya, and a large number of troops, the situation was being contained, but we were not satisfied that we were making sufficient progress in eliminating communist guerrillas. The roads in Malaya were unsafe; acts of sabotage were frequent and our Intelligence services did not indicate that the number of Chinese communists was diminishing. When the security forces had a successful encounter with the guerrillas, those eliminated seemed to be replaced by others.

Now there was the Korean War in which the communists in the North, assisted by the Chinese, hoped to overcome the US-backed South Koreans. HMG had decided to support the South Korean war effort.

At the time of my arrival General Harding was in Hong Kong considering what our contribution to South Korea should be. It was only from the UK forces that units, weapons and equipment could be provided. Gurkhas could not be used. In consultation with the War Office, it was decided that the UK contribution at this stage should be one infantry brigade. This would be commanded by Brigadier Coad, a Brigade Commander in Hong Kong.

While this matter was being considered the French Governor General and C-in-C in Saigon, General Carpentier, asked for an urgent meeting there to discuss the deterioration in Vietnam, where the French were up against strong North Vietnamese forces. It was agreed that I should at once lead an inter-service British delegation to Saigon to discuss the situation with the French authorities. I stayed at Government House and the meetings were a useful introduction for me to the difficult situation in Vietnam.

On my return to GHQ I spent a few days being briefed and then a little time with the C-in-C. He gave me his views on the situation in the Far East, told me what he would like me to do and how he liked to work.

Then there was the Malayan situation to understand. First a visit to General Urquhart at Kuala Lumpur, then a visit to the Gurkha Division and other formations and units. Everywhere I went I was impressed with the operational atmosphere. We were at war with the guerrillas and any visitor felt the determination to get the better of them. Travelling around I used mostly our small Auster planes that could land on the many airstrips that had been constructed near unit headquarters.

By the time Julia arrived by sea with the children, I felt that I was getting on top of my job. John and Mary Harding were extremely kind to Julia and she soon felt at home.

Malcolm MacDonald was the Commissioner-General for South-East Asia and was responsible for political affairs. He sat with the C-in-C's Committee in considering political and inter-service matters in the region. When Harding was away, I would attend the meetings on his behalf. Malcolm MacDonald was a very successful Commissioner-General and set about making friends with the local Heads of State and politicians, particularly in Burma where he gained considerable influence with Ne Win, the President, and perhaps deflected him from an extreme form of communism. He also got on well with the services, but perhaps less well with the local business people. They were accustomed to the more formal methods of a Colonial Governor. MacDonald was very informal with everyone. At a meeting or a big luncheon the guests, as soon as they got in the house, would be invited to take off their coats.

Soon after I arrived trouble broke out between the Moslem population in Singapore and the Dutch community.

During the war a young Dutch girl had been brought up by a Moslem family and had adopted that religion. At the end of the war her Dutch family tried to claim her back. There was a court case and it became a racial issue. The court found in favour of her natural parents. The verdict was announced on the morning of the Commissioner-General's annual conference at his house, Bukit Serene, in Johore, north of the Causeway. Serious disturbances began to develop in Singapore. By lunchtime, it seemed that the situation might get out of hand. I spoke to General Harding at lunch and suggested that it might be as well for me to go back to GHQ at once. He agreed. It was lucky I did so as my vehicle was one of the last to cross the Causeway safely until the late evening.

As soon as I reached Singapore, I went to discuss the situation with General Dunlop, GOC Singapore Base District. We agreed that reinforcements from Malaya were required, so I went on to GHQ and issued the orders. I then got in touch with General Harding and told him of the situation. By that time the Causeway was closed and I had to arrange for armoured cars to re-open it and to escort those most concerned, General Harding, the Governor of Singapore and a few others. It was decided that there should be a meeting at Government House at 9 pm that evening to consider the situation. At that stage there were large armed gangs roaming the streets and no European was safe.

The speed events could get out of hand on a communal matter was a lesson to me. I found the drive in a jeep from my own house to Government House that evening very unpleasant. Later the sudden appearance of large numbers of British troops on the streets of Singapore sorted things out and by the morning the situation had begun to settle down. It had been a nasty experience.

Like so many service families, we had an education problem. We decided to send Joanna to an Army boarding school in the Cameron Highlands, not far from Kuala Lumpur, where we could visit her. The teaching was under charge of the Army Education Corps and of a good standard and she was happy there, although she would have preferred a school in England. We sent Simon to a private preparatory school in Sussex and arranged for him to come to Singapore for the summer holidays. Brian, who was only six, would stay with us.

There were plenty of off-duty activities in Singapore. There was an excellent social club, the Tanglin Club, which provided tennis, squash and swimming; also dancing two or three evenings a week. In addition there were two good golf clubs, cricket and every other imaginable game. The C-in-C had a comfortable launch which gave the possibility of picnics on Sundays to the islands near Singapore.

Although all of us at GHQ were extremely busy, when there was a chance to get away there were pleasant things to do. The Cameron Highlands and Fraser's Hill provided a welcome change of climate which helped to keep one fit. The High Commissioner in Malaya let us use his bungalow at Fraser's Hill, which we always enjoyed. His excellent servants looked after us. It was in connection with one of these visits that a sad tragedy occurred.

A message arrived one evening from Sir Henry Gurney's staff asking whether we would mind leaving a day early. It was obvious that the High Commissioner was coming up himself. We were happy to do so and got safely back to Singapore. We had very strict rules for movement of vehicles and escorts. When a general went anywhere such as Fraser's Hill, he had to have two armoured cars, one just in front of his car and the other immediately behind. Both had to be in touch all the time. Sir Henry, coming up to Fraser's Hill after we had gone down, had two armoured cars manned by the police. Perhaps the men were less experienced than our soldier escorts and got separated too far from Gurney's car. A guerrilla ambush had been waiting for several days at a dangerous part of the road. The ambush was well-organized and a note book recorded all the cars that had passed, including ours on the downward journey. They were evidently waiting for the High Commissioner in person. He was ambushed and killed. Fortunately his wife, who was with him, escaped.

General Harding was due to go to Ceylon the next morning. He had not been well and, in addition to seeing the Governor of Ceylon, he was to have a few days' leave in the hills. His personal staff and I succeeded in persuading him not to change his plans.

Accordingly, the Army arrangements for Sir Henry Gurney's funeral and the enquiries and review of security arrangements that followed fell to the GOC Malaya, in conjunction with myself representing the C-in-C. Sir Henry was much respected and liked in Malaya.

It was now 1951 and the situation in Vietnam was deteriorating badly. General de Lattre de Tassigny, who had taken over command there, came to see General Harding. The French were pressing for support from the US and ourselves, but, with our commitments in Malaya and the war in Korea, there was little we could provide. The Americans were happy to offer an extension of their training teams, but that was not really the full extent of the French needs.

General Harding's time in the Far East was now coming to an end. He was about to be the next Commander-in-Chief in Germany and was to be replaced in Far East Land Forces by General Keightley.

Early in 1951 Julia's parents came from New Zealand to stay with us. I think they found the climate rather trying and her father became unwell and had to go into the army hospital. He was full of praise for the hospital and staff. He liked going round the different beds and talking to the other patients of all ranks.

Soon the Keightleys arrived and it was a very busy time for us all. In view of further French requests in London, it was decided that there should be a conference in Washington between the French, Americans and ourselves on what could be done to help the French in Vietnam. It was decided that I was to represent the C-in-C, and should go via London where I would take with me to Washington the Colonel in charge of the War Office Far East Branch.

At that time Lord Knollys held an advisory post at the Embassy in connection with economic affairs. The Knollys very kindly invited me to stay instead of going to an hotel.

The conference lasted unduly long but I believe that the French felt that it had been useful in that we and the Americans had been alerted to the seriousness of their problem and, for their part, they understood the extent of our own commitments.

Anxious as HMG was that the communist forces should not gain control in Vietnam, it was not our policy that we should become militarily committed there. We had already increased our contribution in Korea and had our hands very full in Malaya. The Americans had explained the type of advice and training they were prepared to give and our own position was now quite clear. I returned via London and was able to report to the War Office on the conference before returning to Singapore.

During my short stay in England, I was commissioned by Julia to visit Southover Manor School in Sussex where we hoped Joanna would go as soon as possible. She was now 13 and ought to become established at a school in England. I saw the Headmistress and she took me all over the school and introduced me to some of the girls.

Now it was back to the many problems of the Far East. We had not been making the progress we had hoped in the Malayan Emergency, and it was decided that a Director of Operations should be selected who would concentrate his whole effort on studying the Emergency and dealing with it.

General Templer was appointed. He was to be given all the resources he wished. His first request was for General Hugh Stockwell to be his No 2. General Stockwell was at that time commanding the 3rd Division, the Strategic Reserve Division, and had recently been sent to Egypt where the Egyptian Government had abrogated their treaty for the location of British troops on their soil. All British forces were now in the Canal Zone. Our relations with Egypt were not happy and it seemed that the situation could deteriorate at any time.

I was appointed to succeed General Stockwell in command of the Division. There were few divisional commands in the army at this time and this was a great step for me.

Everything then began to move very fast. General Templer wanted Stockwell as soon as possible; a successor had to be found for me. I had to have a few days in England to attend to our own affairs before joining my Division in Egypt. I had a few meetings at the War Office and then I set off in an RAF plane for Fayid, the RAF station in the Canal Zone. I arrived there just before midnight and found Hugh Stockwell waiting in the Station Mess to hand over the Division to me. We were less than an hour in the process. Handing over a Division is mostly a matter of handing over personalities. We all have different ways of running things. Hughie could tell me a few of the problems he had met but wisely said that I must sort things out for myself. My Command, in addition to the Division, included the Canal Zone from Ismailiya northwards to Port Said and the north end of the canal. The 1st Division was responsible for Fayid southwards to Suez. GHQ was at Fayid.

CHAPTER XIX

Command of the 3rd Division

During the First World War the 3rd Division had been christened the Iron Division. Monty had commanded it with great distinction at the beginning of the Second World War. I was proud to have succeeded to the command of such a Division.

As I set off in the middle of the night from my meeting with Hugh Stockwell, I had plenty to think about. I had been warned that my accommodation at Divisional Headquarters was rugged in the extreme. It certainly was. My staff liked to tell me that, in pre-war days, my HQ had been the Moascar garrison detention barracks. Imagination may have gone into this description but one could certainly say that, for a Divisional Headquarters, the accommodation was modest. My bedroom consisted of a rather small room with a verandah leading to my bathroom; this consisted of four canvas walls with poles, chest-high, stuck into the sand!

The 3rd Division had been sent out in a hurry when the situation in Egypt was tense. All my units were under canvas except for the Scots Guards who were in good accommodation at Port Said. There were few amenities for anyone. The whole Division was living and working under active service conditions. The wives and families had been left at Colchester, the town on which the Division was based.

A rapid visit round my units, the day after my arrival, showed the important part morale would play in keeping the men happy. They needed to appreciate the importance of the job we had been sent out to do and also that every effort was being made to improve their accommodation and provide reasonable amenities. They needed to be kept busy both with training and sport.

General Festing had just arrived to take over from General Erskine who had been appointed to command in East Africa and get on top there of the Mau Mau problem. Both Generals fully understood the need to get the Division better housed and were extremely helpful.

As regards our operational role, I shared with the Royal Navy a security task in the event of trouble. We had joint plans for action in various circumstances. I accordingly kept in close touch with Admiral Edwardes, the Flag Officer 2nd-in-Command of the Mediterranean Fleet who was my opposite number in the Planning. He always put me up at his house in Malta and entertained me most generously.

It so happened that my first visit to Malta coincided closely with the passage of Julia's troopship through the Suez Canal on her way back from Singapore. I was thus able to travel with her as far as Malta, making a pleasant break for us both. I stayed with the Admiral at Malta and took the opportunity to visit the Highland Light Infantry, one of my 3rd Division Battalions stationed there.

One of the Division's worst headaches in the Canal Zone was the large Base organization at Tel el Kebir. This had been built up during the war and contained vast quantities of stores and weapons, attractive from the point of view of thieves operating on a large scale as well as petty pilfering. The guarding of these stores fell to my Division. Every conceivable device was used on the perimeter fences, and patrols would be active all night, but the thieving gangs were very cunning and skilled and from time to time had their successes.

In addition to my troops in the Canal Zone, I had units at various locations on the North African coast. The Devonshire Regiment under Paul Gleadell was at Darnah. Paul and I were old friends. We had been at school together, also in the 6th Airborne Division and at the War Office, when I was Director of Plans. I had my Armoured Regiment at Tripoli. I visited all these units in their turn and as a result learned a good deal about the North African campaign. One of my Gunner Field Regiments was located in Cyprus, the other two had been left in England, but I was able to visit them when they had their Practice Camp at Larkhill. The RAF would provide me with an aircraft when I visited units in the Middle East theatre.

One of my Brigades, under another old friend, Brigadier John Tweedie, was located in Kenya to contribute to getting the Mau Mau rebellion under control. While they were in Kenya they remained under me for administration, but were under the operational command of General Erskine.

I enjoyed my visits to Kenya; my Brigade was spread over a wide area and I was able to see a lot of the country. When I was at Nairobi, I used to take an occasional evening off to visit the splendid game reserve, which was only a short distance from Nairobi, and in which, if one was lucky, a large sample of the wild life of Africa could be seen.

Not long after my arrival in the Canal Zone I woke up one morning to hear that during the night there had been a *coup d'état*. The King had been deposed and replaced by General Neguib, with Colonel Nasser as his Chief of Staff. I got in touch with General Festing and it was agreed that I should go to Port Said and see the Egyptian Governor and get as much information as I could. The Governor was very agreeable, but I found that he knew as little as I did. He was equally surprised by the *coup*. After calling on the Scots Guards and telling them as much as I knew, which, frankly, was nothing, I went back to General Festing's HQ. We were both astonished at the speed with which the King had been overthrown and Neguib and Nasser had installed themselves, all with a minimum of fuss and, as far as we could make out, few casualties.

Training was an important part of our life. The desert provided a splendid opportunity and I spent a good deal of time visiting the battalions at their exercises. The 1st Parachute Battalion was included in the Division and it was nice to find that my wartime memory of the outstanding quality of the officers and men still held good.

During my time we had two large-scale Divisional exercises in the desert south of Fayid. The most important was code-named 'Triangles' after the Divisional signs of the 1st and 3rd Divisions. The Divisions were matched against one another. It is seldom that a Divisional Commander has a chance to put his Division against another. Not surprisingly, we each of us reckoned, when the exercise was brought to close, that we had out-manoeuvred the other!

After I had been in the Canal Zone for about six months a number of married quarters became free and it was possible for some of the wives to join their husbands. This made all the difference to the lucky ones. I was allocated a major's married quarter in the Moascar Garrison. It may not have been very magnificent, but we were together again. There was a small garden in which Julia was able to amuse herself. Having a house also meant that we could have the children out for the holidays. In those days they were flown out from the UK at the father's expense; there were no assisted passages for children's holidays.

Outside the garrison boundaries, great care had to be taken over security. Even on the main roads along the Canal there was the threat of ambush or other terrorist action. We always had to have an escorting jeep. Julia found that a soldier in a jeep behind her with a machine carbine pointing in her direction took some of the pleasure from bathing and other expeditions! In Moascar we managed to get some rather rough polo. We played on a stony parade ground, which was rolled beforehand but soon cut up and we were always galloping in a cloud of dust.

In 1953 General Harding had become CIGS and paid us a visit in the Canal Zone. He had come to see what could be done to improve the living conditions. The problem of a double garrison using the same living accommodation as a much smaller one was not something that could be overcome quickly but General Harding showed that every possible effort was being made.

When I went to visit my Gunners in Cyprus, Julia was sometimes able to come with me and the Governor was kind enough to ask us to stay. This made a pleasant change from life in the Canal Zone. Occasionally I could manage a few days' leave. Kyrenia was a favourite place, particularly in the spring when the wild flowers were out on the hills. They were a wonderful sight, cyclamen on the north slopes and anemones on the south in great profusion.

When I was in England on one of my visits to my Gunners at Larkhill, I had a message that the CIGS wanted to see me at the War Office. General Harding gave me the news that I was to be the next Director of Military Operations at the War Office.

This is generally regarded as one of the best Directors' jobs in the War Office and certainly the most interesting. The DMO works very closely with the CIGS and has the Director of Plans under him. This was particularly nice for me as General Harding had had me as his Chief of Staff in the Far East and had now chosen me for his DMO.

I went back to the 3rd Division in great spirits. While I was at the War Office it had been suggested that I should see as many of the difficult areas in the Middle East as possible before taking up my job as DMO. In conjunction with the Middle East Command, I therefore planned a number of tours. First I went to Jordan to see General Glubb Pasha and the Arab Legion. Julia was invited by Glubb Pasha to come with me so that she also could see some of the sights.

We flew to Aqaba and from there drove to Maan. On the way we passed through the most amazing clouds of locusts; the sky was thick with them. It was impossible to see clearly out of the jeep. It was like going through a blizzard of snow with large solid flakes. This went on for miles. One could understand the damage to crops. We spent the night at Maan as guests of the Jordan Government.

The next morning we set off for Petra. We were to see the famous 'Rose Red City, half as old as Time'. The ancient city is approached through a narrow 'sik' or gorge with high rocky sides. At the entrance we changed from the car to ponies and rode along the sandy bottom, quite dry, with the old water channel cut in one side of the wall. As one approaches the end of the sik, the magnificent spectacle of the treasury comes into sight with all its startling colours. We then rode on and saw the other famous monuments and the temple on the heights.

From Petra we went on to Amman where we were entertained by the Arab Legion. The next day I was fully committed with visits to units of the Arab Legion.

While we were in Jordan General Glubb Pasha arranged for us to have a tour of the Jordanian sector of Jerusalem. We took in a short visit to the Dead Sea on the way; it was interesting but not attractive.

The Jordan Government had taken over a building in the Old City as an Official Guest House and we stayed there. Some said that it had been a convent, others a harem, but whatever its history, it was a beautiful house, with lovely painted ceilings and fine furniture which had been chosen with skill and taste. Anyone visiting the ancient quarter, which, in those days, was in the Jordanian part of the City, could not help being fascinated by the biblical character of the people and of the narrow streets with animals wandering about.

Some of the buildings were a disappointment, in particular the Church of the Holy Sepulchre. This church, going back hundreds of years and venerated by all the different Christian faiths, seems to be spoilt by the attitude of the different Christian sects who use it, each competing with the others and different services taking place at the same time.

I think that Julia and I got most pleasure from the Mosque of Omar and the Dome of the Rock. A religious atmosphere seemed to prevail in those places, side by side with the magnificence of the building. It had been a wonderful experience and it makes one sad to think that the Old Quarter of Jerusalem and the West Bank is now no longer Jordanian territory. Then we were on our way back to Amman to say goodbye.

The next visit that I did took me to Iraq and the oil-rich Gulf states. Julia was not able to come with me, but Dick Hull, the Chief of Staff to the C-in-C Middle East Land Forces, was anxious to make the trip so we went together. We started with a visit to Baghdad and stayed with the Ambassador, Sir John Troutbeck. The political situation was delicate and it was useful to hear the Ambassador's view on the future.

Baghdad itself was disappointing. Perhaps the romantic legends made one expect too much. Most of the city gave the impression of dilapidation and neglect. The Embassy and its grounds were a refreshing exception.

The flight down the Euphrates to its junction with the Tigris at Basrah was interesting; then on to our next stop at Kuwait. The oil boom had already started and great new concrete buildings were beginning to spring up. It was interesting to see the speed with which a new modern city could be built with Western skills and local labour.

We flew on from Kuwait to Bahrain. Here we were looked after by the Political Resident, Persian Gulf, who took us to call on the Ruler. He was enjoying great wealth and we were received with considerable ceremony. Bahrain was then the political and business centre of the Gulf, as well as being oil-rich, and its position was well established. Next we went to Abu Dhabi, an emerging state which we were supporting politically, militarily and financially. Sheik Said, the Ruler, was being squeezed by the neighbouring states, which realized its potential wealth. Shortly before we got there, a dispute had developed between these states and Abu Dhabi over ownership of the Buraimi Oasis. It was decided that we should visit the Oasis accompanied by Sheik Said, who was anxious to obtain British support for his claim. The landing strip was only suitable for the type of light aircraft which the RAF maintained at Sharjah and we set off accordingly, accompanied by Sheik Said. At Buraimi the Sheik developed with some force his arguments for his claim which had been disputed by Saudi

113

Arabia and Oman. We then had to cope with an enormous banquet that had been prepared in a big tent. The food was good, but we sat on the floor facing the Sheik, with our legs and feet in the opposite direction. This meant sitting twisted in a most uncomfortable position, very vulnerable to cramp. Only the right hand is used for eating. We then returned to Sharjah and started our journey back to the Canal Zone. Aqaba would be a stopping place.

En route one of our two engines began to give trouble and eventually had to be shut down. It was very inhospitable country down below, and there was some anxiety. It was suggested that our load might be lightened by throwing overboard the carpet I had bought at Baghdad! I did not agree that this would be a good idea and fortunately it did not become necessary and we landed safely at Aqaba.

My last six months with the 3rd Division were exceedingly busy. It was the height of the training season, which, that year, included another large-scale exercise. A great deal of advance preparation was always involved in such an exercise but the effort was well worth it.

The long-term future of our garrison in the Canal Zone was at that time much in our minds. The large Base Depot at Tel el Kebir continued to be difficult to protect. Its future in particular was the subject of a lot of thought and study. The H.L.I., which had been in Malta, had been moved to Tel el Kebir. They did a good job there, even though they did not much like it. They were a particularly high-spirited unit and could get into a little trouble in too close contact with other units.

I found the handover of my Division a sad occasion. I had completed the two years in command which General Harding had promised me and had enjoyed every minute of it. Command of a Division, however, is a very special job and it was hard to leave.

It had been proposed to me at the War Office that, before coming home, I should visit the territories of Northern and Southern Rhodesia, as they were then known. Southern Rhodesia was a particularly important territory in East Africa. Their armed forces, although not large, were efficient and had made a valuable contribution to the Commonwealth during the war and since. I decided that I should make these visits after I had handed over command of the Division and then return directly to England, thus saving time and avoid cutting the visits short. I would have a lot to do before taking up my appointment at the War Office.

I left the preparation of my tour programme to the local military authorities. I let it be known that I was happy to do whatever they thought would be useful but that it should be a business visit and I would not be able to fit in more than a minimum of sightseeing. Perhaps I made this a little too definite, as the South African Military Authorities invited me to visit them after I had finished in Rhodesia, but the Rhodesian Authorities, who were in charge of my programme, refused on the grounds of lack of time. I would have enjoyed a South African visit and was sorry to have missed the chance.

My handover in the Canal Zone completed, I flew direct to Salisbury. Southern Rhodesia was then an important and stable country with a distinguished and much respected Prime Minister, Mr Huggins, who had the political and economic affairs of the territory in good shape. I visited most of the military establishments and was able to let them understand how much we had appreciated their help. At one time they had sent a unit to Malaya.

I could not finish my visit to Rhodesia without seeing the Victoria Falls. This magnificent sight needs to be seen again and again from the many different angles where a spectacular display of rainbows can be seen. Flying in one sees from a distance the great plume of spray in the sky which is the first indication of the Falls. Then from the ground there are countless walks to produce different views.

I spent the night at the Victoria Falls Hotel and then crossed into Northern Rhodesia the next day. The Kariba Dam had not been built when I was there, but its planning and the sharing of its use was a main subject for debate. At that time Northern Rhodesia was prosperous, with the price of copper high. It was, however, a one-product economy and when the price of copper dropped the territory suffered considerably. Copper had been so profitable that tobacco and other farming products had been neglected.

I was now at the end of my East African visit and I took an aircraft bound for England. It was a Comet. The Comets had been having trouble. Several had been lost without explanation. En route for Cairo, orders came through that all Comets were to be grounded. There had been yet another unexplained disaster. It was certain that at Cairo there would be a pile-up of passengers from the grounded Comets so I made for the booking office with maximum speed, prepared to take a seat to any Western European destination, from which I could then transfer for London. I was glad to accept a flight to Brussels. It was a sad end to the Comets, for they were magnificent aircraft. Their problem was eventually identified, but they never flew again with passengers.

CHAPTER XX

Director of Military Operations

Now that we were back in England we had to decide where we were going to live. Joanna and Simon were at boarding school and I knew that my work at the War Office would be very demanding. We had bought a house at Haywards Heath with the idea that I would be able to commute. I soon learnt that I would have to be at the War Office from early in the morning until late each evening. It would mean an impossibly long day to add a railway journey at each end.

On arrival at the War Office I would need to read through the Foreign Office telegrams before the CIGS's arrival and look through the papers for the day's meetings. I must, therefore, have a room in London. Mrs Seary-Mercer was kind enough again to let me have a room with bed, breakfast and dinner at 64 Cadogan Square. The house we had bought at Haywards Heath was convenient for Julia and for me when I could get home but we did not want to live there permanently. Julia and the family had settled into the Woodford Valley of the Avon and had come to regard that as home.

And so it was from Cadogan Square that I set out for the War Office on my first day. General Harding would be my boss again and I looked forward to serving under him once more.

In those days the principal entrance to the War Office was the Great Door in Whitehall. This entrance, with its marble hall and fine staircase, was reserved for Generals and Senior Civil Servants. The staircase led only to the second floor, where the principal offices were. Half-way up the marble stairs branched and then each part curled round to end opposite the Secretary of State's door. There was a nice story that, when mounting the stairs, a Labour Secretary of State and his junior Ministers would turn to the left, where the stairs branched, whereas a Conservative Secretary of State would turn right!

The CIGS had a fine room and group of offices at the right-hand corner of the building and the Permanent Under-Secretary of State had the equivalent room and offices on the left.

My first morning, as I entered by the front door, I was greeted by the smartly dressed Head Doorman with his top hat. I already knew of the S of S's office pretty well, and that of the CIGS, from my time as Director of Plans and during the war. Now I walked along the passage from the CIGS's to what would become my own room. This room I also knew well from earlier days. It was a splendid room with a great marble fireplace, a large desk and eral deep leather chairs for visitors and other chairs for more formal visits. There was the antique oval walnut table, round which I had sat many times for meetings. On the wall there was row upon row of photographs of distinguished Generals, DMOs of past years. There seemed to be few well-known Generals of the First World War and later who were missing. Before long I realized that meetings and seeing visitors would form a very important part of my life.

My predecessor, Roddy McLeod, was in the room to meet me and with him was the DMO's personal assistant who had been many years in the job. Now my own briefing began. A day with Roddy put me well in the picture on current issues and problems and on the people with whom I would work. General Bill Oliver was the Vice-Chief of the Imperial General Staff and I soon got to know him and to like him very much. He would generally attend meetings I had with General Harding.

The next few days were taken up by briefing from the Colonels of the different Military Operations Branches. First there was MO1, among whose important functions was the handling of the papers on the Chiefs of Staff committee meetings and of those of the Defence Committee of the Cabinet to which the Chiefs were often invited. The Military Operations 1 Branch was also the link between the Joint Planning Staff and the War Office. The second branch for me to see was MO2 which dealt with Far Eastern affairs. They were fully occupied with the Malayan Emergency, the Korean War and with the communist influence creeping into South-East Asia. The US-sponsored South East Asia Treaty Organization was also getting under way; Australia and New Zealand were involved in this. My next engagement was with MO3, responsible, among other things, for the Western European Organization and NATO. Finally, MO4 which dealt with Middle

Eastern affairs. All these theatres were exceedingly active at this time. We have seen how much had been going on in the Far East and the Middle East. Now the Korean War was at last showing signs of coming to a settlement. Negotiations were going on over a frontier between North and South Korea on the basis of the 38th parallel. General Templer's firm hand in Malaya had had a decisive effect there and the worst was now over. It was only in the Middle East that the situation seemed to be worsening. British oil interests in Iran were nationalized in spite of our protests, the Americans having adopted an unhelpful attitude on this. It was felt that US commercial interests and ambitions in the area were playing a big part. The Prime Minister, Mossadeq, had, however, now fallen from power and it seemed that the situation in Iran should improve. The plan for withdrawal of British troops from Egypt and the lease of the base facilities to the Egyptians was going ahead. Our relations with Nasser had, however, not improved. Eden, as Prime Minister, distrusted him.

My average day at the War Office would start at any time before 9 am. At 10 am I would generally have a meeting with the MO Colonels. We would sit round the oval table and discuss the Joint Planning papers which would be considered later by the CIGS and also any Foreign Office telegrams that ought to be brought to his notice. The Director of Plans and I would then go into the CIGS and discuss these papers and others. The VCIGS would join us if he was free.

General Harding was often away on visits and the Vice-Chief would then take his place at the COS meeting. If the Vice-Chief was also away, I would represent the Chief at the meetings.

One of the functions of the DMO in my day was to be the contact between the Commonwealth Military Representatives and the War Office. I had a regular monthly meeting with them and got to know them all well. I would brief them on developments that might be of Commonwealth interest and they could question me. If any Commonwealth representative wanted to see me separately, I always arranged it.

Soon after I took over as DMO the terms agreed with the Egyptian Government over a British withdrawal from the Canal Zone and the leasing to the Egyptians of the Suez Base were finalized. It was decided by HMG that we could no longer afford the cost of maintaining 80,000 British troops in the Canal Zone and that we must pull out. For many years our position in Egypt

119

had been regarded as one of the pillars of our Middle East strategy. The arguments and implications of pulling out were, therefore, discussed back and forth at ministerial level over many months; Nasser was deeply distrusted.

The security of our passage through the Canal and our vital oil interests were factors which made us most unwilling to accept the risk of pulling out. Finance, however, had the decisive say and the decision was taken to leave.

Later in the year the fears of the French and ourselves were justified. The Egyptians, ignoring our treaty rights, assumed control of the Canal and its management. Although the Egyptians undertook to maintain international 'freedom of passage', there was little confidence that this would be guaranteed at times of crisis. The Israeli Government in particular felt that use of the Canal was likely to be denied to them because of the bad relations between Egypt and Israel. They felt that there was little use in attempting to negotiate and they decided to resort to force. The Chiefs of Staff, including General Templer, who had succeeded Field-Marshal Harding as CIGS, felt very strongly on the importance of the Canal. The problem was the action which the British and French should take. None of us had any illusions on the objections the Americans would have to military action on our part. It seems, however, to have been accepted in Government circles that their reactions would not go beyond protest and would certainly not amount to sanctions. Too much confidence seems to have been placed on a 'Special Relationship'.

There was no doubt in London or Paris of the need for action on our part. The Canal must not be overrun by the Israelis, nor must it become a battleground for the Egyptians and Israelis. Freedom of passage for international shipping must be guaranteed. The Israelis were about to take unilateral action to protect their own rights.

It was accordingly decided by the British and French Governments that an Anglo-French Assault Force should be formed and located in Cyprus, ready for any action found necessary. The force was to be commanded by General Sir Charles Keightley. It would consist of all arms and have naval and air support and it would also include British and French parachute units. I nearly became involved in this, General Keightley told me later, as he had asked for me as his Chief of Staff, a post I had held under him in the Far East. He was, however, told that I was not available. I was

13 Julia

14 Julia visiting the Semarang Hospital, Java (see p. 152)

15 "An audience with President Sukarno . . . . The Ambassador . . . . reported . . . . that the President had been at his most relaxed and affable" (p.152).

16 A Farewell to Arms

already heavily involved at the War Office with the composition and preparation of the Force. It was to be a well balanced Anglo-French force capable of taking on any task likely to arise. It was hoped that the existence of this force and its location in Cyprus would act as a deterrent and that it would not need to be used.

In London the political side of these events was handled by a small committee of the Cabinet whose thoughts and proposals were kept strictly secret. Similarly, in the Service Ministries, the possibility of action was handled on a Chief of Staff level.

The matter was brought to a head by the action of the Israeli Government. It seemed likely to them that the Egyptians would indeed close the Canal to Israel shipping and the Israel Government was not prepared to wait. During October, 1956, they despatched a force towards the Canal by way of the Gaza Strip with the intention of seizing the Canal and the Egyptian territory needed to defend it.

The Israeli force was making rapid progress towards the Canal and the British and French Governments decided, towards the end of October, that they could not wait any longer.

Accordingly a 'Requirement' was sent to the Egyptian and Israeli Governments that hostilities must cease within twelve hours, and that all military forces must withdraw from an area ten miles wide either side of the Canal. The Israelis complied, but the Egyptians refused. It was not until the end of October that I knew of the Government decision and the 'Requirement'. General Templer sent for me and briefed me. He then asked me to go to the Foreign Office and establish contact with the Branch dealing with Middle Eastern affairs. I went over at once and found that the same degree of secrecy had been enforced in the FO. The branch concerned were just being put in the picture.

It was now hoped that an air bombardment of military targets would induce the Egyptians to cease military operations. Warnings were then sent out that civilians should be removed from the vicinity of military targets. An early target selected was El Gamil airfield and airforce base. This bombardment took place on the 1st of November. It did not have the effect hoped for on the Egyptian Government, now relying on international support. Accordingly the Amphibious Assault Task Force of British and French units was despatched. The assault was opened by a parachute drop on El Gamil airfield by the British 3rd Parachute Battalion and a French Parachute Battalion dropped on Port Fuad on the opposite side of the Canal. Both these airborne landings were entirely successful. The joint Anglo-French Amphibious Force had sailed from Cyprus to land on the beaches close to Port Said on the morning of 6 November. The landings were completed without a hitch and the force occupied its pre-planned positions.

By this time, however, international objections to the Allied action had begun to mount. The US, acting in concert with the Russians, had raised the matter at the United Nations. The British and French Governments had vetoed the conclusions, but as the US, the USSR and the Arab States controlled the oil supplies, there was furious diplomatic activity among the nations concerned. The British and French ordered their forces not to advance further south and in due course they ordered their withdrawal from Egypt. In the meantime, the Egyptians had blocked the Canal by sinking shipping.

Prime Minister Eden's health gave way and he became too unwell to continue at the head of the Government. He was succeeded by Harold MacMillan who must have been as much involved in the Suez decision as Eden himself.

Those of us close to General Templer at the time realized how deeply upset he was by the Army being sent on a mission well within their capability, then being withdrawn and not permitted to complete it. It was a political disaster that many of us would like to forget.

Busy days followed Suez. The forces assembled for the operation had to be dispersed and efforts made to repair our international relations. The Arab nations had been our friends for many years. Now they were firmly linked to Egypt.

General Templer himself was not very well and had to go into Sister Agnes's for a short time. The Vice-Chief was away and I found myself representing the CIGS at a number of COS meetings. They were particularly interesting ones and I enjoyed the experience. I used to go to Sister Agnes's after the meetings to see General Templer; he had to know how things had gone.

During the autumn I had been told that my next appointment would be Commandant of the Staff College, so my time as DMO was fast coming to an end. I could not have had two more delightful Chiefs than Lord Harding, as he had become, and Field-Marshal Templer. They were real friends and I enjoyed every minute of my time with them. It was sad for me to end with Suez, but happily our relationship with the Arab States began to mend.

CHAPTER XXI

Commandant, the Staff College

The time had now come for me to move to the Staff College. During my period as Commandant it was divided into two wings. Rather more than half the students were in the Main Building at Camberley. The rest were at Minley Manor about three miles away near the Camberley-Basingstoke Road. There was no significance between the two wings. It was the luck of the draw as to which wing students were sent. Minley was a large country house in lovely grounds. It had been bought by the War Department to be used for both accommodation and work. There were a certain number of activities, such as lectures, indoor exercises, dinners and so on, for which both wings would be brought together in the Main Building Minley was a small and more intimate establishment and generally students preferred it to the Main Building. Being in the Main Building close to Camberley had its advantages. The work done at each wing was exactly the same.

The Directing Staff at the Staff College were carefully selected top-grade officers, chosen by the Military Secretary in consultation with the Commandant. A lot of trouble was taken over their selection. They were all officers marked out for advancement.

The senior staff consisted of an Assistant Commandant, during my time Rupert Brazier-Creagh, later David Peel-Yates, and three full Colonels. The Directing Staff working with Student Syndicates were substantive Majors given the temporary rank of Lieutenant-Colonel. There was generally a high percentage of married officers among both the DS and the students. The DS were generally accommodated in married quarters in the grounds of the Main Building. The students rented their own accommodation. The bachelors had good rooms within the wing of the Staff College to which they belonged.

I had Staff College House. This was a large comfortable house, only a couple of hundred yards from the Main Building. It was well furnished by the Ministry of Works, except for the big dining-room, which had no furniture. It suited us that the dining-room was empty as we were glad to furnish it with our own things. We needed to entertain a good many visitors, for the night as well as for meals. Staff College House was well equipped for this and ample servants were provided. Altogether we were going to be very comfortable. The Haywards Heath house was not really what we wanted and we sold it.

I took over Commandant in January, 1957, and, at the outset, followed the programme I had inherited.

Special emphasis was put on syndicate work. The students were put into syndicates of about ten in each at the beginning of each term and then worked together throughout. During some of the exercises the students would take it in turn to fill the various appointments on a staff. One student would be appointed to act as the Divisional or Brigade Commander and so on through the different staff appointments, ending, perhaps, with a Staff Captain. Individuals would change their jobs at the end of each exercise so that all had the chance of exercising different levels of responsibility.

Lectures and addresses by prominent soldiers and civilians also featured in the programme, but the practical side of working as a team is what counted most.

I had a very good link with the Commandant of the French Ecole Superieure de la Guerre, General Lecomte. He and I became close friends. Julia and his wife were equally good friends. They stayed with us on a number of occasions and we stayed with them in France. General Lecomte took me on several extended visits. An interesting one was in the Toulouse district. Before going to Toulouse and Castres, the General had met me off the train at Marseilles and then took me on a tour of most of the Cote d'Azur. We were driven at breakneck speed in a large Citroen. When we had 'done' the coast, we went inland to Arles in Provence. There we were met by the Maire and I was shown the sights of that fine Roman City and then to Les Baux de Provence all in one day, for a stop at Hotel Ousteau de Beaumanière with its three stars for excellence. There was a splendid dinner waiting, but by that time I was exhausted and I had lost my appetite. My bed was calling.

The next morning, before making for the Toulouse area, we did a quick tour of the Carmargue, famous for its bird life and the wild white ponies. General Lecomte did not want me to miss anything.

Then we set off for Castres, near Toulouse. I was already pretty tired by the time the exercise started, but it had been an interesting experience. At Castres I was put up at the Prefet's house and next morning I started meeting French officers and talking to them about the exercise. While visiting the exercise, extra sight-seeing visits were added such as an hour or two at Albi, to see the splendid collection of Toulouse-Lautrec paintings. I have quoted this French visit in some detail to show the immense kindness and hospitality I received everywhere in France. It took a lot of living up to when the lecomtes came to us at Camberley.

Meanwhile the Staff College programme was going ahead. In between lectures and syndicate work, there would be an occasional big exercise in the country where the problems which we had dealt with indoors were presented more realistically outside. There again the students took it in turns to play parts from the Divisional Commander downwards.

A lot of work by the Directing Staff was involved in the preparation of these exercises. Mostly they were passed on from course to course but tailored each time by the views of the Commandant. The exercises were made to follow as realistically as possible the events of each battle.

A particularly valuable feature of the Staff College course was the annual battlefield tour in Normandy. The Staff College had built up an excellent team of 'guest speakers', or 'guest artists' as we called them. They were wartime Commanders from each battle studied, from Divisional down to Company and Platoon Commanders. They brought into the battles we were studying the 'atmosphere' of the battlefield, vividly describing their thoughts and reactions as an engagement was described. One of the battles studied during my time at Camberley was General Tiny Barber's 15th Scottish Division battle west of Caen, codenamed 'Epsom', chosen as an example of the essential contribution by the junior officer in battle. General Barber always came himself and he and his team gave a splendid presentation.

The battlefield tour always included the great Armoured Corps battle east of Caen, codenamed 'Goodwood', fought in July, 1944. The declared intention of this battle was to pin down the German armour in the east and thus help the American breakout in the west. I had been witness to this battle during the war from the early stages when the bombers, in vast numbers, pulverised the German position. This bombardment was then followed by the advance of three armoured divisions supported by massed artillery.

I sat in an upstairs window of a farm building on the Troarn Le Mesnil ridge and could see it all as the assault developed. When the tanks got beyond the range of much of their artillery support they were devastated by the concealed 88mm guns of the Germans and the bazookas hidden in the corn. I had my own opinion on this battle and found the presentation by the tank commanders and others fascinating. This battle has always produced fierce controversy on whether Monty had hopes of breaking through on the east flank or whether his only aim was to draw the German forces away from the right flank of the bridgehead before the American breakthrough in that sector began. The students, as well as the Directing Staffs, had lots to say about this.

Finally we studied the operations of the 6th Airborne Division on 6 June, 1944.

A full day was allotted to each of the operations, the students being divided into three groups. Unfortunately, in my day, we did not have the advantage of German participation, as was the custom later.

At the end of each day the DS and students were pretty tired, but they had enjoyed themselves. There was one snag and that was the very poor accommodation for the students. The DS were in a good hotel but the students lived in dormitory conditions. In spite of that, at the end of the day we all found a way of enjoying ourselves. General Tiny Barber was indefatigable. He always took a party of DS and others to Deauville to gamble and brought them back late at night. I was not very enthusiastic about this adventure as the DS worked hard and must be at the top of their form the next morning. However, everyone survived. As regards the comfort of the students, I am happy to say that I was able to arrange for the next year's course to be accommodated at Cabourg, a pleasant sea-side town with small hotels. I had left by the time the change had taken place, but I am told that it was popular. It was certainly more convenient for Tiny Barber and his gambling!

Without doubt the great feature of my time at the Staff College was the visit of the Queen, accompanied by Prince Philip, Christopher Soames, the Secretary of State, the CIGS, General Templer, and members of the Queen's staff. It took place on St George's Day, 23 April, 1958. The visit was to mark the centenary of the Staff College. The Queen wished to see something of the ordinary work of the College and follow a programme as close as possible to a normal working day. Her Majesty sat in at a series of syndicate discussions. We chose from the normal Staff College syllabus subjects that we thought would interest the Queen. The Royal Party broke up and visited the syndicates separately. The discussions were quite uninhibited and there was plenty of wit and argument. The Queen went to several different syndicates and followed the discussions with great interest. I was told that, some months later, Her Majesty quoted with great accuracy something that had been said at one of the discussions. At the end of the morning the Queen met and talked informally to a large number of Directing Staff and students. After this there was a luncheon that everyone attended, including Directing Staff wives.

This Royal visit was soon followed, for me, by one from Princess Alexandra to the Durham Light Infantry. I had become Colonel of the Regiment in July, 1957, and on Saturday, 17 May, 1958, we were to celebrate our bi-centenary. Shortly before this event the Queen had appointed Princess Alexandra to be Colonel-in-Chief of the Regiment.

Princess Alexandra had kindly consented to come to Brancepeth Castle, our depot, and take part in a parade to honour the occasion. This must have been one of her first Royal engagements.

The Princess looked charming. It was a very demanding ceremony which involved inspecting rank after rank of soldiers and saying a word to the men here and there, adding up to a great many words. The weather was most unkind and her light coat did little to protect her. On and on she went and those of us taking part realized how bitterly cold she was, but she never flagged and completed the parade as though she was enjoying a summer day.

At the end of the Parade I led the Princess into the Great Hall of the Castle where an enormous fire was blazing. One realized then just how cold she was, and what an ordeal it had been.

On that first occasion the Princess captured the hearts of us all - and has retained them ever since. As Deputy Colonel-in-Chief of the Light Infantry she still attends major Light Infantry events and gives us all great pleasure.

We must now return to Camberley. The students worked hard but not too hard. I believe that a little earlier the pace had been altogether too hot. Some students lived in a state of perpetual anxiety as to whether they would make the grade or be returned to their units. I remembered my days as a student when I might have burned the midnight-oil perhaps once or twice during my entire year. The work was well within the capability of us all. I remember feeling that much of the value of the year was learning to work together as a team. It was the object of our emphasis on syndicate work.

This was the substance of my opening address. I expected hard work but I wanted it done with smiling faces and I wanted the students and their families to enjoy their time at Camberley, as we had done in our day. I believe that they did enjoy it.

The Staff College Reunion, at which past and present students met, was an annual occasion. We would have a few guests for lunch at Staff College House and meet many more during the day. I remember Lord Ironside lunching with us at the start of one Reunion. The Duke and Duchess of Gloucester were with us on another occasion and met a large number of past and present members. HRH had been a 10th Hussar in bygone days and much enjoyed military occasions.

Another interesting feature of the year was the annual visit by a selected team of headmasters from some of the larger public schools. The headmaster of Downside, who, as a boy had been at school with me, came one year and was able to tell me his off-the-record views on the other headmasters. He was, in fact, very useful and had lots 'of ideas. He told me that the headmasters were very impressed by the quality of the students and the technique of the instruction. We welcomed any suggestions they might have.

Each term we had a number of dinners, often organized by the students, who would select and write to the individual they wished to meet or to hear speak. I remember particularly an evening with Lord Alanbrooke who had been CIGS when I was Director of Plans. His diaries, edited by Arthur Bryant, had just been published. They were not appreciated by Winston Churchill who had expressed his displeasure to Brookie in a very frank manner.

An interesting guest was the German General Hans Spiedel, C-in-C Allied Land Forces in Central Europe. He had been Chief of Staff to General Rundstedt on the Russian front. He was to spend the night with us. He had addressed us in the morning and he needed to be entertained during the afternoon. I wrote to Lord Freyberg, who was Governor of Windsor Castle, to ask whether it would be possible for him to be taken over the Castle. Lord Freyberg organized the most splendid tour for us, to which Julia also came. We had the Director of the Queen's Library to take us round. As the Queen and Prince Philip were away, we were able to see many things not normally on view.

During June I had a charming letter from Field-Marshal Templer telling me that I was to be promoted to Lieutenant-General and appointed GOC-in-C Southern Command. I was to take over from General Bobbie Erskine on the 1st of November, 1958. This was well beyond anything I could have hoped for. There were some 80,000 troops in Southern Command and my responsibility was to include, in addition, the UK Strategic Reserve. I would be responsible for their training and operational command. Their administration would be in the hands of the local commanders of the areas in which they were located.

My headquarters would be at Wilton and Julia and I would live at Bulford Manor, a charming house with the Avon flowing at the bottom of the garden.

I was sad to leave the Staff College, but this appointment was better than anything that at that stage I could have dreamed of. I was most grateful to Gerald Templer.

I remained at Camberley until the end of the summer term, which was a convenient time for the change of command. I then had a period of leave before taking over from Bobbie Erskine.

CHAPTER XXII

Southern Command

On the 1st of November, 1958, Julia and I motored down to Bulford Manor and took over my new Command as GOC-in-C Southern Command from General Sir George Erskine.

Southern Command included Aldershot District, with Major-General R. Bramwell Davies in command and proud of the title 'Home of the British Army'. 'Ronny' Bramwell Davies was a very able officer, but, sadly, had not been very fit which had affected his promotion. Major-General John Cubbon was commanding South-West District, with Headquarters at Taunton, and Major-General 'Geordie' Gordon-Lennox was now commanding the 3rd Division which had been my former Division. Aldershot District was relatively concentrated but Cubbon's District was spread over the South-West and also had an important Territorial Army element. He had a Regular brigade at Plymouth.

In addition to the operational units in the Command, most of the Army Schools were located there and I was responsible for their administration. These included the Royal Armoured Corps at Bovington, the Royal School of Artillery at Larkhill, the Royal Signals at Blandford and the School of Infantry at Warminster. Each of these had their own Major-Generals at the War Office responsible for their policy and training.

We had a large number of Territorial units in the Command, many of whom were first class. The Wiltshire Yeomanry were outstanding. They were difficult units to get into and they could pick and chose both their officers and other ranks.

Southern Command also contained most of the big depots and Service Establishments such as those at Donnington, Bicester, Childwell and others. Geographically we covered Buckinghamshire, Oxfordshire, Gloucestershire, Hampshire, Dorset, Somerset and the whole of the South-West.

I was very lucky to have a splendid Chief of Staff, Major-General 'Slim' Heyman, to help me in taking over the Command. He had been with Bobby Erskine for some time and was very much on top of his job.

Julia and I were to live at Bulford Manor. Bobby Erskine had done some research on its history and had decided that the oldest part was 14th century. There was also a large wing that was certainly Elizabethan, with a rather unreliable ghost said to inhabit it. I don't know of any guest who complained, but Slim Heyman always refused to sleep there. In addition there was a Georgian wing and an ugly Victorian wing, where our own rooms were.

The large area covered by Southern Command and the many units and establishments to visit could have been a problem, but I was lucky enough to be able to get a helicopter whenever I needed one. This made all the difference when, for example, visiting the Brigade at Plymouth or other distant units. It more than doubled the amount of country I could cover in a day. In the summer, when there were a large number of T.A. camps, everything was made much easier by using a helicopter.

The Regular Brigade located at Plymouth was a great advantage in building up a good liaison with the Royal Marines and Royal Navy. The Naval C-in-C, Plymouth, put me up on a number of occasions. I also kept in touch with the Naval C-in-C at Portsmouth, Admiral 'Lofty' Power. When I paid my official call on him, he had a Guard of Honour formed up beside *Victory*.

Many important overseas visitors used to come to the schools and establishments in Southern Command. King Hussein had been at Sandhurst and was anxious to refresh his memories and also to see something of the 16th Parachute Brigade. The King saw the modern techniques of dropping heavy equipment by parachute and he watched some of the training.

My time at Southern Command coincided with the decision to discontinue National Service. Commitments in the operational units overseas and in the ordnance and other depots at home had only been made possible by the large numbers of National Servicemen available. The first stage would, therefore, need to be a reduction in our commitments; only then could the rundown begin.

An early decision was to substitute, as far as possible, civil labour for National Servicemen in the large depots of the ordnance and other establishments. This policy, once agreed, could only be introduced gradually.

The intake for the Army schools would also have to be reviewed. Much of this was naturally a matter for the War Office but the repercussions were felt everywhere in the Army. A big reduction of this sort was obviously unsettling on officers and men of the regular Army. With 80,000 men in the Command, there would be a morale problem. Careful planning and gradual change helped the process to run smoothly. Although the abolition of National Service had barely got underway during my time at Southern Command, the planning put considerable pressure on the Staff.

One of the important administrative problems during my time related to accommodation, particularly married accommodation. The availability of quarters was quite inadequate for the number of men and their families. As a result there was great hardship over separation, which had been going on for a long time. Large building projects were at last being undertaken at Tidworth, Bulford and Larkhill, both barrack accommodation and married quarters. Aldershot was to be virtually rebuilt. Unfortunately the married quarters, and particularly the officers' ones, were not being built to anything like pre-war standards in size or quality and there was a War Office requirement on the number of houses to be built to the acre of land which resulted in people being rather overlooked. The most important thing, I agreed, and I believe rightly, was to get the families which had been separated, sometimes continually since the war, united. Lengthy arguments on the number of houses to the acre could only delay this. The barracks in the Command were now hopelessly out of date. Many of the hutted camps were of First World War vintage. Permanent accommodation was urgently needed.

Soon after I arrived the Quartermaster General told me that he was sending the architect for the rebuilding of Aldershot to see me. I believe that he was a distinguished man in his profession and had done a lot of work on the rebuilding of Coventry. When he had taken his plans from their many containers and spread them on the table, my staff and I were horrified. It is a matter of taste whether or not a series of flat-roofed bungalows appeals, but it seemed to us that the needs of the modern army were not understood. There was the small matter of car parking. Already in 1958, almost all Warrant Officers and many NCOS had their own cars and these had to be parked in the barrack area. Any thought that cars could be permanently parked on a parade ground was quite unrealistic. That was just one small example of how the modern Army was not understood by civilian experts. Quite naturally the architect had little knowledge of the peacetime Army. The general appearance of the proposed buildings may well have been good modern design but were not what the Army needed. Seeing the remains of the buildings today makes me think that, although our comments were very amateur, they were not unfounded.

The new Command Headquarters at Wilton was, fortunately, in an advanced state of construction. We were pretty satisfied with the type of two-storeyed building being provided in that area. When I first took over command, my office and that of the Chief of Staff was in Fuggleston House, close to Wilton; the remainder of the Staff were in hutted accommodation in the grounds. Towards the end of my time, the Chief of Staff and I moved over to the new accommodation which was purpose built and very convenient. Gradually the rest of the Staff moved over to the new accommodation as it was completed.

Salisbury Plain was the main training ground for the Army in the South of England. It was only there that large-scale exercises could be held; some 90,000 acres of land had been purchased at the beginning of the century. Parts of the area were leased to farmers with varying tenancies. Some tenancies allowed grazing rights only and there were pennings into which stock could be driven during an exercise. Other tenancies required prior notice from the Army of troop movements over the land and there were some farming leases of land which could only be used for training if the Manoeuvre Act was applied. The land was used extensively by troops in the Command and, for large exercises, troops from elsewhere might be brought in. The War Department lands were under control of the Lands Branch at the War Office, but we were anxious to maintain good relations with the farmers and the Lands Branch would arrange an annual meeting for us with them and we would have lunch together afterwards. Tanks and heavy army vehicles inevitably did damage to the land but we did our best to limit this. There was always the problem of gates and fences. In my experience, what the farmers most wanted was permission to plough up more land. I was assured on countless occasions that they would be happy to accept damage if it occurred. We, on the other hand, could not agree to this, knowing that soldiers would not drive tanks or vehicles over fields of barley. A photograph in the newspapers of them doing so would put the Army in an impossible position. The land was essential to us. Amesbury Council waged a constant war to recover the village of Imber which had been requisitioned during the war and the population moved out. The village, however, was still in frequent use as a training area for village fighting. It is now little more than a skeleton.

Our other training areas in the Command were not trouble-free either. We had certain training rights on Dartmoor, an area most carefully defended by preservation societies. Soldiers would frequently be accused of leaving litter and a cigarette packet would be sent to us as evidence. Aldershot was such an old-established Army station that we had less trouble there. Bovington and Lulworth had their own training area problems. I have no doubt that it is much the same today.

During my time in the Command we had a big exercise in Tripoli of particular interest. The object was to put into practice the reinforcement of an overseas garrison in an emergency. The whole force was to be transported by air and to be maintained from the stores and ammunition they could take with them, plus a very limited resupply by air. Their transport also would be limited to what could be taken with them. Both Lord Mountbatten, Chief of the Defence Staff, and General Festing, Chief of the General Staff, attended the exercise and regarded it as a most valuable one which had brought out important lessons on scales of equipment for the type of task selected.

I was Colonel of the Durham Light Infantry throughout my time at Southern Command and one of my regular engagements was to visit Durham in September each year for our Old Comrades Reunion. This took the form of a parade and inspection by the Lord-Lieutenant, followed by a march past and then a service in Durham Cathedral. Lord Lawson, the Lord Lieutenant, never missed the occasion. As a working miner, he was much loved by the people of Durham. He was a good friend of ours and came to stay with us while I was at the Staff College. At home in Durham, he lived very simply in a miner's cottage which he had had most of his life.

The D.L.I. had made an outstanding contribution during the War. Seven D.L.I battalions had come out at Dunkirk in 1940, three battalions were together in North Africa, and five battalions fought side by side in Normandy. There was hardly a Durham family that did not make its contribution. Whenever one talked to a local man, be he a porter, miner or policeman, there would be one thing in common, that he or a close relation had been with the D.L.I. during the war.

Southern Command had always kept in close touch with the Royal Air Force and from my Airborne Forces days I felt particularly closely associated with them. I had quite an amusing experience when I went to address their Staff College at Andover. It was during the winter and it had been snowing during the night, and the weather conditions got worse as I set off in my car. When we reached Beacon Hill, some three miles from the house, I found that the moderately steep slope was choked with cars that could neither get on nor turn back. I was jammed in the middle. I was most anxious as I did not want to let the RAF down. It would have been very bad for the Army Commander to miss his engagement. Suddenly out of the sky popped a helicopter. The pilot took a run up the halted traffic, turned and landed by the door of my car. He asked whether he could help. He certainly could and he lifted me to the RAF Staff College to the amazement of my hosts who reckoned that it was not flying weather and that there was no chance of my meeting the engagement. It was one up for the Army. At that time there was a struggle going on for the RAF to take over all the helicopters.

The reader will understand that the Army Commander Southern Command led a full life. His military commitments kept him more than fully occupied, but it was also important that he should get to know the local people and become involved in the sporting and other activities of the Command. The Territorial Army, which was splendidly represented throughout my very large area, was a useful link. It was particularly important during this period as we were in the midst of a major reorganization of the T.A. The changes being introduced were often unpopular as they involved in some cases the amalgamation of very distinguished yeomanry and other regiments. I tried to go to the meetings of the Territorial Associations of the different counties in the Command so that I could hear of the problems which the War Office proposals sometimes caused and make representations if appropriate. I could also explain the reasons for some of these proposals. The T.A. Associations were often chaired by the Lord-Lieutenant of the County and they could help a great deal in obtaining agreement.

The local people were very friendly to Julia and me. We had

certain roots in Wiltshire, first during the war, when I was Commanding the 5th Parachute Brigade, and then, while I was away in the South-East Asia, the Baileys helped Julia to find a house. While I was still abroad they arranged for her to have what is now called Lake Rising. Julia was well established there, with Nanny and the children, when I came home from the Far East to be Director of Plans. We eventually had Lake Rising on a 20-year lease and thought of it as home, although, in fact, my various postings abroad prevented us from enjoying it as much as we would have liked.

When I came back as Army Commander, people were wonderfully kind to us and we received many invitations. I was invited to hunt and to shoot in this very sporting area of Wiltshire. The Gunners at Larkhill kept a horse for me in their stables and I had many splendid days with all the local hunts.

Unless there was some big exercise or other occasion, I tried to keep Saturdays free for sporting activities. Lord Margadale, as he now is, was particularly kind to us both. He mounted me countless times on his splendid horses and I had many very enjoyable days with the South and West Wilts, of which he was Master. I also had many invitations to shoot. Freddie Bailey was very generous with shooting invitations. Charlie Tryon would ask me to shoot and a day at Wilton or at Longford, with the partridges, would be a special treat.

During our second year at Bulford Manor, our daughter Joanna became engaged to Peter Sebag-Montefiore and they were married from Bulford Manor. I was a very proud father as I led my extremely good-looking daughter up the aisle of Bulford Church. Julia's mother and father came from New Zealand for the occasion.

CHAPTER XXIII

C-in-C FARELF

My next appointment, that of C-in-C, Far East Land Forces, suited me admirably and I was lucky to get it. I was to take over from General Dick Hull who was to become Chief of the Imperial General Staff in succession to General Festing.

It was agreed that Julia and I should go by sea to Singapore early in April, 1961, and spend only a short time in taking over so that Hull could also return by sea. A sea voyage made a pleasant break in between two busy jobs.

Flag Staff House, where we would live, was already well known to us. It was a large and comfortable house. The bedrooms were air-conditioned and the drawing-room and dining-room were large airy rooms but air-conditioning was unnecessary. There was a big garden and grounds and a tennis court. A guard-room was at the entrance to the drive with accommodation for the guard. The guard was provided in turn by the different units in Singapore. There was a short ceremony at sunset each evening when the Union Jack was lowered.

Lord Selkirk was the Commissioner General and we soon became good friends with him and Wendy Selkirk. My service colleagues were Admiral David Luce, Naval C-in-C, and Air Chief Marshal Selway, the Air C-in-C.

Lee Kuan Yew was the Prime Minister and Dick Hull had arranged a meeting with him to say goodbye and to introduce me. Unfortunately the meeting had to be cancelled at short notice and I did not get another opportunity until a month or so later when I was staying at the Cameron Highlands Hotel. Looking out of my window in the early morning, I saw Lee Kuan Yew putting on the golf green in front of the Hotel. This was my opportunity, so I went down and introduced myself to him and asked if he would like a game, he agreed and we had a pleasant morning together.

Golf was quite a feature of life in the Far East. Confidential discussions were often held during the course of a game. In this way the Press and unwelcome interruptions were avoided. I remember a game during the negotiations for the establishment of Malaysia which resolved into a discussion between Lord Selkirk, Tunku Abdul Rahman, Prime Minister of Malaya and Lee Kuan Yew. I was present to make the four but kept in the background.

When I went out to Singapore this time the Malayan Emergency was virtually over, but we still kept careful security arrangements in force. Any relaxation could have resulted in trouble. The force levels in Singapore and Malaya were not very different to those when I left in 1952. The Gurkha Division was now commanded by Major-General Walter Walker. There was a Commonwealth Brigade, including Australian and New Zealand units, located at Terendak. There was still an Armoured Car Regiment and much the same number of infantry battalions as in 1952.

General Sir Rodney Moore had a special appointment, directly under the Malayan Government in Kuala Lumpur, as GOC Federation Army. The Federation Army was being built up and our aim was to help them in every way. I therefore kept in close touch with Rodney and one of my first visits was to him and his wife at K.L. Rodney's wife kept a gibbon in the house which ran loose where it liked.

I soon visited Roddy McLeod in Hong Kong, which was under my command. Roddy was an old friend and I was delighted to have him at Hong Kong. I knew that he would solve any problems that arose there. At that time illegal immigration from mainland China was putting a great strain on the civil authorities. The police were fully stretched and the Army had to make its contribution. Illegal immigration was not on the same scale as in Hong Kong today, but it was none the less a heavy burden on the security forces.

The Chinese Government objected to illegal immigration as much as we did and our measures against it proved a point of contact with the Chinese border guards. There were other strange contacts with the Chinese. For example, they provided the drinking water supply for the whole colony. The relations between the civil administration and the Army had always been good, and with Roddy in command I had no doubt it would remain so. The GOC Hong Kong had a special position in the colony. He was a member of the Governor's Executive Council and he held other honorary positions.

★　　★　　★

Fairly early in my period of command Harry Hohler, the British Ambassador at Saigon, invited me to stay to discuss the situation in Vietnam. When the French pulled out after the defeat at Dien Bien Phu, there was little of the old administration left, though President Diem remained in office. He was an able man, but he had inherited an impossible task. The Army needed complete reorganization. The police force was in an equally poor state. There was no trained Intelligence organization. Worst of all, the President was in dispute with the Generals on the tactics that should be employed against the Viet Cong guerrillas.

I readily accepted Harry Hohler's invitation as this was the part of South-East Asia in which there had been the most serious deterioration in the political and military situation since I had left in 1952 and I needed to get myself in the picture as soon as possible. This visit proved to be the first of a number which I paid to the Ambassador during my period in command. On each of these visits the Ambassador took me to see President Diem. I think that the Ambassador valued the opportunity of being present at my audience and hearing an account of the situation direct from the President. As I visited Vietnam a number of times, it enabled us both to follow the course of military events as they developed. I always also made a point of calling on the two Generals who seemed to have the most influence in the Army. General Doung van Minh and General Kim, both of whom had no hesitation in voicing to me their discontent with the existing command system and the tactics proposed by President Diem. In my day Minh was an important figure in the Army. President Diem must have known that I was seeing him but did not seem to mind and was frank in telling the Ambassador and me of his difference of opinion with the Generals.

It was in November, 1963, that General Minh launched his military coup which deposed President Diem and resulted in his death. Minh assumed the Presidency himself but only lasted a few months before he himself was deposed. Minh was a likeable man but he never seemed of presidential quality. I had left South-East Asia before General Minh's coup took place and do not know the full details. I was, however, sorry that the Americans had not been able to help Diem more. He seemed far the ablest man in the political field and his successors did not measure up in any way. Perhaps the future American disasters resulted to some extent from the absence of a good Vietnamese leader.

It was during my period in South-East Asia that the US Assistance Command began a massive build-up in the quality and quantity of their assistance. General Harkins was the Chief of the Assistance Command and was also the Commander Designate of the South-East Asia Treaty Organization, to which the Australian and New Zealand Governments belonged. I always had a full briefing from General Harkins and his Staff when I was in Saigon. The Americans were also very kind in providing me with aircraft or helicopters, so that I could see the mountainous country in the East and other areas where Diem had told us that the Viet Cong were building up their strongholds.

During this period of American assistance, the advice they were giving seemed entirely sound. As far as I could discover there were no American ground units deployed on operations at this time. They were, however, giving substantial support in the air. In conjunction with the Vietnamese Army, they had also had set up a Ranger school modelled on our Jungle Warfare school. They were most anxious to take full advantage of our experience in Malaya and I was taken round the school on several occasions.

As time passed, the information I gathered on each visit seemed to indicate a steady worsening of the political and military situation. On one rather extended visit, the Ambassador asked whether he could take advantage of the travel arrangements that had been made and accompany me. I was delighted to have him with me as it gave us a chance to discuss the situation more fully.

Now it was necessary for me to spend some time in Singapore. After a visit of some days away from my Command there would inevitably be a considerable pile-up of work for my return.

Singapore was still a major UK Overseas Base. There were large installations for the holding and repair of a variety of stores and equipment, weapons and vehicles and for the maintenance and distribution of medical and other technical supplies which would be required to maintain a large number of troops and be ready for any eventuality. The Commanding Officers were justifiably proud of the condition in which their stores and equipment were kept and of the way in which they defeated the adverse weather conditions.

★   ★   ★

The time soon came round for another overseas visit. We kept in close touch with the Thai military authorities so I chose Thailand. The Thais were rather shut in by the Communist threat from Vietnam on one side and Burma on the other. Ne Win, as President of Burma, had had strong communist leanings but, by the time I was in Singapore, he had become a close friend of Malcolm McDonald, Lord Selkirk's predecessor as Commissioner General, and had shifted his political position considerably to the right. Whether or not on account of the uncertain situation on their frontiers, the Thai Army was particularly friendly to us. When, therefore, I had an invitation from the British Ambassador at Bangkok, Sir Dermot MacDermot, to visit Thailand and to stay with him, I readily accepted. I was anxious to maintain the link that had been established with the Thai Army, more particularly as at one stage during the Emergency we had felt that the Chinese communist guerrillas were using an overland route from Thailand to infiltrate into Malaya. We were keen, therefore, to maintain our friendly contacts with Thai Service personnel and were glad to welcome visits to our schools and establishments, and to reciprocate by visiting theirs.

Thailand is a very beautiful place, the temples outstanding in their richness. We were taken to see some of the more spectacular ones. The Thai Army also arranged for us to visit the King's Summer Palace, some two hours' journey north of Bangkok.

We were flown along the Thai frontier and realized what a difficult border it would be to protect. On return to Bangkok, I had the opportunity to discuss with the military authorities their problems on this frontier and elsewhere.

Early next morning, we were taken to see the floating market. The stalls are either built up on poles or the products are displayed in open boats and much of the vegetables and other foodstuffs for the city passes through the market. We were then taken round the stalls in a motor boat.

Finally no visitor to Bangkok is allowed to leave without making a shopping expedition. Everyone buys the beautiful Thai silks in charming colours and it is certainly good quality silk. Needless to say, we did not leave the shops unscathed.

The only thing we did not enjoy about Thailand was the size and ferocity of their mosquitoes. There was every possible protec-

142

tion at the Embassy, but they always won. There was a continual buzz inside one's mosquito net at night.

★　　★　　★

Having spent some time in Thailand and learnt of their anxiety over their frontier with Burma, I was glad to accept the invitation of our Ambassador in Burma to visit him and see something of the country on that side of the border. After the war Burma had become an independent parliamentary democracy, outside the Commonwealth. Shortly before I went there, however, parliament was suspended and a Revolutionary Council of Senior Officers, under Ne Win, took over power.

It was arranged by the Ambassador, Gordon Whitteridge, that I should see Ne Win at the start of my visit. Just before my meeting with him, Julia and I had been to see the Shwedagon Pagoda in Rangoon. It is a magnificent temple, and I knew that I would be expected to make a donation to the priests in charge. The donation expected was in accordance with the rank of the donor. The Ambassador told me that £20 would be expected from me. This was thirty years ago and was rather more demanding on the pocket than £20 today.

When I saw Ne Win later in the morning he was in excellent form and very welcoming. Almost the first thing he asked me was how much the priests had got out of me. When I told him, he was very amused and reckoned that I had been skinned. Ne Win had been weaned from extreme communism and was very agreeable. He appointed one of the senior officers of his Revolutionary Council to accompany me for a tour of Burma. He took us for a splendid tour, using a Burmese Army aircraft. We were entirely in the hands of our Revolutionary Council Member who was a Brigadier. Among the places he took us to was the Inle Lake, where the fishermen have a curious method of rowing. They stand up in their boats and use one leg instead of a rowlock to support their oar.

We then went on to Taunggyi to call on the Commander of Eastern Command. We dined with him and spent the night there. The next morning we went on to Mandalay. At Mandalay there was another magnificent pagoda and again the performance of making a donation to the Pagoda priests.

We spent the next night at Maymyu and in the morning I visited the Services Academy. The commandant gave us lunch after which our party left for Anisakan by car and joined our aircraft for the journey back to Rangoon and then on to the Embassy. The next day we left for Singapore after a most useful visit.

January and February were, for obvious reasons, a popular time for visitors from the U.K. to want to come to stay with us. We did our best to head them off Chinese New Year but were not always successful. Everything in Singapore closed down during that period, the servants did the minimum and most of the shops were shut. There are processions in the streets and other festivities among the Chinese community. We often had to accept visitors as Singapore might be one stop en-route for Australia or elsewhere. Thus we returned from Burma with a busy programme ahead.

★　　★　　★

A visit that all C's-in-C enjoyed was to Nepal to inspect our Gurkha set up there for the recruitment and preliminary training of the Gurkha soldiers. When we made this visit the RAF provided an aircraft, Julia came with me and we also took one of the officials from the Commissioner General's Office who had business with the Ambassador. As we approached the Himalayan Range from the direction of Calcutta we had our first full view of the magnificence of the snow-clad peaks. The pilot circled several times to give us the full benefit of the view.

Our establishment in Nepal consisted of a recruiting staff in the hills, and the training organization in the plains below.

We were met at the airport and taken to the Embassy. The next morning we were briefed on the system of selection and recruiting of Nepalese applicants who greatly exceeded the numbers which could be accepted. We also had explained the system of looking after and paying our pensioners who are widely scattered in the hills.

An arrangement had been made for me to have an audience with the King of Nepal. In the afternoon Julia and I had a chance to see something of Katmandu and its temples and bazaars. The Ambassador had a cottage along the route to Mount Everest and he took us there the following day. Almost all the way there was a splendid view of the mountains. I think that what we enjoyed most about the trip was the stream of Nepalese, men, women and children, all heavily loaded, who passed us on the route, making for Katmandu. Their loads seemed to be mostly foodstuffs for sale in the market. Beside the road every piece of land that could be cultivated was in use and terraced to prevent the soil being washed away by the rains.

On the following morning, after saying goodbye to the Ambassador, we went down to the plains to inspect the Gurkha recruit, reception and training establishment. Before the Gurkha recruits were accepted into the British Army they had to have health and fitness tests. Their suitability had also to be assessed. There were plenty of applicants to choose from. Only those likely to make good soldiers were accepted and passed down to our Gurkha units and establishments.

The Gurkha Depot at Dahran was well set up and I was impressed with the quality of the officers and their enthusiasm. This enthusiasm permeated the whole depot, being passed on to the Gurkha recruits. Altogether my visit to Nepal and the Gurkhas proved most useful.

★　　★　　★

One of the highlights of our time in Singapore was a visit to Cambodia. We flew to Phnom Penh and after official calls and an audience with Prince Sihanouk we flew north to Siem Reap to visit the fabulous Angkor Wat. Siem Reap was a small country town with an hotel, a railway station, a few shops, an airport and, most important of all, a road to Angkor Wat.

We set off by jeep, belonging to the Cambodian army, and soon saw Angkor Wat standing in a plain cleared of jungle and surrounded by a moat and approached by a causeway with a balustrade of carved Nagas (snakes) and a huge multi-headed Naga at either end.

Angkor Wat was begun early in the reign of Suryavarman II, King of the Khmers, between 1113-1150. It is about one mile from the ancient capital city and had been beautifully reconstituted by the French during the 1920s. The bas-reliefs on nearly every wall are amazing and beautifully carved. Hundreds and thousands of apsaras (temple dancers) in various poses cover the walls and, of course, records of the triumphant battles. As it is a temple, there are, besides, many religious scenes. The Royal Regiment of Elephants is also well represented — they were a trump card in earlier wars. The lotus bud towers soar above the rest of the building.

There are many other wonderful temples nearby of which the Bayon at the new capital of Angkor Thom is the most remarkable. The capital was moved to Angkor Thom after the disastrous defeat of the Khmers by the Chams of Siam. Jayavaraman VII, who reigned towards the end of the 12th century, was very advanced for his times and built over 100 hospitals, well staffed with doctors. He also built the Bayon, an architectural wonder with great towers on the four sides of which were immense portraits in stone of Buddha, in fact of himself whom he believed to be the reincarnation of Buddha!

Alas, Angkor has been overtaken by more recent wars in that unhappy country and, when last I heard, it was no longer possible to go there and the jungle was rapidly reclaiming it.

A visit to Korea was another important one. The South Koreans, supported by the Americans, held a firm position on the 38th parallel. When I visited Korea there had been no fighting for some time. The North Koreans, supported by China, and the South Koreans, by the Western Allies, balanced one another, but the situation was delicate.

I was shown the frontier positions in detail; the South Korean defensive positions had been built up in considerable strength. On both sides of the 38th parallel the opposing forces were thoroughly on their toes.

I also spent a good deal of time being briefed by the US Staff about the contribution they could make in an emergency and on the relationship between the American and South Korean armies. It was clear that both the US and South Koreans were well prepared against a surprise attack. The earlier fighting had been hard and was a warning on how quickly things could deteriorate.

The political position in Korea, at the time of my visit, was very unstable, but, in spite of this, the Korean Army and officials were very friendly.

Our Ambassador in Tokyo, Sir Oscar Morland, had invited us

to visit him. He made arrangements for me to meet the Chief of Staff of the Japanese Army and other senior Japanese Generals, who in turn arranged for me to see as much as possible of the Army, their training methods and schools. I was glad to have the chance of discussing their methods with them; they had made remarkable strides in the short time since they had been permitted to re-arm.

In addition to the sightseeing plans that the Ambassador and his staff had made for us, we decided to go for the weekend to the Fujiyama Hotel where I remembered staying during my visit 25 years earlier. Everything was greatly changed; it had expanded into a luxurious hotel and was extremely expensive. It seemed to cater almost exclusively for American tourists. They all wore badges with their names, and, without having badges ourselves, we were frequently asked what tour we belonged to!

There had been a great deal of building on the slopes of Mount Fuji since 1935, which to me spoilt its character. Also the excessive tourist development everywhere had spoilt a beautiful scene. However, we enjoyed our walks and the comfort of the hotel. We found little that we wanted to buy, even if we could have afforded serious shopping.

On our way back to Tokyo, it had been arranged that I should visit a new car factory assembling British makes of car. I was intrigued to see that several different makes of British car were being assembled on one production line but all seemed to be going smoothly. There was only one union in the factory and it was interesting to hear that the work force expected to be employed permanently with the firm. There was no casual labour and everyone seemed very happy. It was all very different to Japan's mass production methods of today.

Indeed, Japan had changed radically from my visit of 25 years earlier. Now Tokyo was a prosperous modern city with a mass of luxury hotels, high buildings and broad streets. To me, however, the Japan I saw on this occasion had lost the charm it used to have.

★   ★   ★

Soon after the Tokyo visit we had a short holiday of an unusual sort. The Commissioner in Sarawak was kind enough to arrange for us to go in his launch up one of the great rivers of Sarawak and spend the night in an Iban longhouse. These longhouses are built on stilts beside the river. It was a fascinating experience. We were made very welcome by the Ibans. The longhouse accommodated much the same number as a small village, all living a communal life. Our hosts had screened off a small area for us to sleep in and to dress, but that did not prevent the little prying eyes of the children from making holes to see what their strange guests were doing.

We all ate together, a meal consisting mostly of fish, and after the meal the Ibans sang their songs. The river provided the very elementary washing and other facilities. It was a delightful experience.

In the morning the Commissioner came back in his launch to pick us up and we set off again upstream. The river ran through beautiful country with thick jungle on either side. Down by the water's edge people were washing themselves and their clothes, repairing or improving their longhouses and their fishing nets. The birds and the monkeys overhead provided a continuous chatter. We felt very close to nature. We stopped at the outpost where the Commissioner had spent the night. His official gave us tea and refreshments and told us about life on the river. Then we went on upstream to see an impressive waterfall. Finally we turned for home, going peacefully downstream to the Commissioner's house.

Close liaison between the UK forces and those of Australia and New Zealand has always been a feature of our policy. Our soldiers have fought alongside one another during two World Wars. During peace our organization, training and equipment has been maintained along the same lines. The readiness with which we could count on our Commonwealth friends to hurry to our assistance was shown once more by the support they gave us in Malaya by the despatch of the splendid Commonwealth Brigade Group of Australian and New Zealand units, to take part, alongside our own UK units, to defeat the Chinese communist guerrillas.

The exchange of officers of our three Commonwealth countries has proved a most successful means of strengthening our already close ties. This exchange takes place in all the more important schools and training establishments, such as those for the

Armoured Corps, the Artillery, Engineers, Infantry and so on. An officer in any of the Commonwealth Armies, if selected for a course at, for example, the Staff College, may undergo his course at Camberley or alternatively in Australia, Canada or elsewhere and obtain exactly the same qualifications.

At GHQ, Farelf, we felt particularly closely in touch with Australia and New Zealand, our neighbours. We greatly valued the Brigade Group they had placed under our command in Malaya, and we enjoyed the visits of their senior officers to see their troops in the field and to discuss the policy we were following.

Like previous Cs-in-C, I was invited by the Military Authorities of Australia and New Zealand to visit them, see their schools, establishments, and their training, and to meet their officers. Our High Commissioner at Canberra, Lieutenant-General Sir William Oliver, was an old friend. I had served under him as Director of Military Operations when he was Vice-Chief of the Imperial General Staff and we had got on well together. I was much looking forward to seeing him again. I decided that I would fit in a visit during the autumn of 1962.

Our first stop was at Darwin in the Northern Territory of Australia to rest the crews and refuel. The Administrator of the Northern Territories, Mr Nott, was kind enough to put us up. He gave a big dinner for us. Many people had motored a considerable distance; indeed, we were told that some of the guests had come from as far as Alice Springs. A party was a rare occasion!

From Darwin we went to Brisbane and then were driven to the Australian Jungle Warfare School at Kanungra. Some very good demonstrations were arranged. The Directing Staff had obviously had a good deal of experience in Malaya and knew their job. I spent a most interesting and useful time at the school with a very enthusiastic Group Directing Staff and students. Our two Jungle Warfare Schools kept in close touch and we had evidently profited from one another's ideas and experience. We spent the night with the Brigadier in Charge, Brigadier Wade. He gave us a splendid dinner, but was disappointed not to be able to offer us 'Mud Crab', a considerable delicacy, and he pressed us to stay with him on our return journey to Singapore. He assured us that we would be eating something very special. We of course accepted his invitation. When the time came we found ourselves confronted with large numbers of crabs staring up at us from our plates. We managed all right for a bit, but by degrees the crabs began to win.

Our host had taken so much trouble that we would have hated to disappoint him. We struggled on but eventually had to give in.

From Brisbane we went to Canberra and met a very warm welcome from the Olivers who had invited us to stay. General Oliver had arranged a Press Conference for me that evening, the Press being very interested in the achievements of the Commonwealth Brigade and particularly the excellent reputation of their own Australian units. They had every reason to be proud of them. Later that evening the Olivers had invited to dinner a cross-section of political and military personalities and it made a most interesting introduction for me on Australian affairs.

The next day I had a number of official calls to pay. Lord de L'Isle, the Governor General, was unfortunately away. Oliver had also arranged a tour of the work on the Snowy Mountains Development Scheme. The purpose of this was to increase the supply of electricity to Sydney by the development of a hydro-electric system using the water of the Snowy Mountains which was being diverted, by extensive tunnelling, to a number of power stations in the area. After passing through the hydro-electric system, the water would be used for irrigation purposes.

Bill Oliver also arranged for me to visit Woomera, a desert area used for training. On our way back we came across a very large kangaroo. I had not seen a kangaroo of that size before and the officer who was with me stopped the car, hoping that the animal would show its paces, but the kangaroo stood staring at us from a short distance. We wanted to see it move and my guide said that, if he got out of the Land Rover, it would move off at once. He then got out and started to move towards the kangaroo, but, far from moving away, the kangaroo started to advance towards him. I am glad to say that the officer decided to withdraw; it seemed that the animal did not wish to be disturbed! Soon the kangaroo decided to move off and it was a wonderful sight to see this large animal hopping gracefully over the desert.

From Canberra we moved on to Melbourne where General Dallas Brooks, the Governor, had invited us to stay. There was a large dinner party the first evening and much talk of cricket and racing which are great features of Melbourne life.

Next we went to Sydney, again staying at Government House, where General Eric Woodward was Governor. I had a considerable programme of military visits at Sydney. I spent a morning at the Staff College which seemed to be organized very much on the same lines as our own. I met our British Service Officers and also visited the Cadet College.

The next day we set off for Adelaide. We both thought this a most charming place, not unlike an English cathedral city. I had talks with General Bastyan, the Governor, whom I had known before. We were impressed with the South Australian wines and Simon Furness, my ADC, was able to arrange with his opposite number to buy a few cases for us to take back to Singapore. It did not seem to taste quite the same when we got there, but we enjoyed it none the less, and it brought back happy memories of our visit.

Now our aircraft headed for New Zealand, to land at Christchurch. We stayed with Julia's cousin and her husband, Hester and John Elworthy. John had been in the Royal Navy but had retired to farm outside Christchurch. I visited various units and we met a number of officers and their wives at a large evening party.

After two days we flew on to Wellington where General Bill Thornton was waiting to greet us. He was an old friend and was at that time Chief of Staff of the New Zealand Army. He was an excellent host and I enjoyed going round different establishments and schools with him and meeting New Zealand officers. I also met our own British officers who were on exchange appointments and I had the opportunity to find out whether or not we were sending the type of officer who fitted well into N.Z. units and schools. We then moved on to Hawkes Bay to stay with Julia's father and see some of the other members of her family.

I took a few days off before joining Bill Thornton again for an exercise and to see training at Waiuru Camp in the centre of the North Island.

I ended my New Zealand tour with a visit to the Prime Minister, Mr Holyoake, who was accompanied by the Minister of Defence. I was able to thank Mr Holyoake for the splendid work done by the N.Z. Battalion in Malaya and tell him of the high reputation they had acquired.

The Commissioner General, Lord Selkirk, was anxious to improve our contacts with President Sukarno and the Indonesian Authorities. He and the Ambassador, Sir Leslie Fry, therefore proposed that I should start the ball rolling by paying a visit to the Indonesian Army, if that was acceptable to Sukarno.

All went well and Julia and I duly set off on 28 October, 1962, for Djakarta in an RAF Aircraft. General Jani, the Commander-in-Chief, and a large contingent of representatives of the Armed Forces, together with some Foreign Military Attachés, were formed up to greet us at the airport. A Guard of Honour had also been mounted.

After a short interview with the Press, we were installed at the new Hotel Indonesia, where it had been decided we should stay as the guests of the Commander-in-Chief. That evening we dined quietly with the Ambassador at the Embassy so that I should have an opportunity of being briefed. I told the Ambassador of my previous experience in Java, when commanding in Semarang in central Java, while my Parachute Brigade were the garrison there. The Ambassador suggested that, if questioned on this, I should say that I was there in connection with the surrender of the Japanese Army.

The following day was devoted to a round of calls including an audience with President Sukarno. The Ambassador, who accompanied me, reported to the Foreign Office that the President had been at his most relaxed and affable. I felt that this reception set the tone for the rest of my visit. That evening the Ambassador gave a large reception for a broad section of the Indonesian service officers and civilian officials, as well as members of the Commonwealth and American communities.

The Indonesian authorities had allotted one of their aircraft to me for our tour. The following day we set off in this aircraft, accompanied by a senior Indonesian General. It was indeed a whirlwind tour which we had in front of us. Our first stop was Semarang. I was delighted to be back again but of course made no mention of my previous connection with the town, nor did my hosts mention it. I was received everywhere with the greatest cordiality and hospitality. At Semarang I called on the Commanding Brigadier and was shown the sights and the military installations. Everything looked in good order, but much changed after nearly 20 years. Julia had a different programme. She visited the hospital and, from my old photographs, she is also sure that she was taken to see the house where I had lived during my time there.

From Semarang we flew on to Bali where we were to spend the night. Soon after we arrived we were taken for a short tour. Most of the men and women were in their local and very attractive dress. In the evening we were treated to what was called a cultural entertainment. The background was a Javanese traditional play with some local dancing added. At the end there was a big supper party, mostly European food, probably for our benefit, but also some fish dishes. Bali was not in those days swamped by tourists as it is today. It was a quiet and attractive scene and our hotel, close to the sea, was very pleasant.

Next we flew to Surabaya, an important town on the north coast of Java. It was there that Brigadier Mallaby had been ambushed and shot in 1945. Now the atmosphere was as friendly as everywhere else. The General gave us lunch in the company of about a dozen of his officers, after which we flew on to Djakarta, from where we visited the ancient temple of Borobodur. This is an enormous square temple in the same style as the temples at Angkor Wat in Cambodia. Borobodur provides a link in the history of Indonesia with that of the powerful Khmer Empire of the 14th century in Cambodia and is an important Indonesian monument. Next I had a military appointment to see the National Military Academy and inspect and address the students. I spoke to them on leadership and apparently my address went down well, its success being reported on by the Ambassador in his despatch for the Foreign Secretary.

Next we flew on to Bandung, in the hills some distance from Djakarta. Here we called on General Adjie and his wife, who came from Jugoslavia. General Adjie arranged a picnic for us close to the Tangkuban Crater after which I watched an infantry training demonstration and then went on to the Command and Staff School. There I was able to tell the students about our own Staff College. They were particularly interested in the emphasis we put on syndicate work. All the students appeared to speak good English.

The next day we visited an Indonesian arms factory and then the cavalry training centre. Finally we were taken to the parachute and commando training centre. I had plenty to discuss with them and I think that we were able to interest one another.

Now it was time for home. We flew to Djakarta where my own

aircraft was waiting. There was still another Press Conference and more speeches to complete with. Julia made a speech saying how much she had enjoyed everything that had been arranged and how she looked forward to returning one day. General Jani said with evident sincerity from across the crowded room, 'Any time you like. Just give me a ring and I will be at the airport to meet you!'

These many visits I made to foreign territories were hard work but at the same time they were fun. I was assured by the different Ambassadors of the political importance of the visits and their invitations were always most kind and pressing. Our Ambassador at Djakarta, Sir Leslie Fry, wrote in his despatch to the Foreign Secretary: 'The visit can have done nothing but good to our relations between the British and Indonesian armies, and indeed to Anglo-Indonesian relations generally'.

It is curious that this visit, which took place towards the end of 1962, was followed, after only a very short time, by a complete break in our relations with Indonesia. This was because of the establishment of Malaysia. The territories of Sabah (British North Borneo) and Sarawak were included in the new sovereign state of Malaysia. These same territories were claimed by Indonesia.

Troublesome small-scale fighting took place between Malaysian forces supported by the British and Indonesian forces which made border incursions into both East and West Malaysia. This border fighting began early in 1963 and continued until a settlement was reached in 1966.

Almost my last act as C-in-C, Farelf, was to visit our troops in Brunei and Sarawak during the early stages of the dispute.

CONCLUSION

When Lord Mountbatten became Chief of the Defence Staff, he decided to appoint an overall C-in-C to command the three Services in each Command. The Far East Command was to be a Naval command with an Admiral as C-in-C. Admiral Luce, who had been my opposite number as Naval C-in-C, was to be the overall C-in-C. When he was due for relief it would be by another Admiral. This meant that my job would cease to exist.

This was a sadness to me but I had had a wonderful career and enjoyed every minute of it. On leaving, I had many charming letters, including one from Field-Marshal Montgomery.

These chapters perhaps show how lucky I have been to serve under so many distinguished officers, whose friendship and help has enabled me to enjoy my life to the full. Julia and I were given a wonderful send-off by all ranks of GHQ and from our many friends in the Far East. The help that Julia had given to me and to many people and their families throughout our service had been immensely appreciated.

Now our hope is that the Army will continue to offer to our successors as much interest and fun as we have enjoyed for more than thirty years.

Index